ENJ

Enjoying God

ANDREW BRANDON

KINGSWAY PUBLICATIONS
EASTBOURNE

Unless otherwise indicated, biblical quotations are from the
New International Version, © 1973, 1978, 1984
by the International Bible Society.

Front cover photo: Tony Stone Photolibrary—London.
Cover design by Peggy Chapman

British Library Cataloguing in Publication Data

Brandon, Andrew
   Enjoying God.
   1. Christian life—Devotional works
   I. Title
   242

   ISBN 0–86065–686–1

Printed in Great Britain for
KINGSWAY PUBLICATIONS LTD
1 St Anne's Road, Eastbourne, E Sussex BN21 3UN by
Richard Clay Ltd, Bungay, Suffolk
Typeset by Nuprint Ltd, Harpenden, Herts.

Many thanks to Beth Capey for putting the typed manuscript of the book into a word processor, and thanks to Elaine March for her secretarial assistance during the editing of the manuscript.

Many thanks to my parents, my wife, Tom and Ivor Powell, the Revd and Mrs Luland, Les Isaac, and the host of other men and women of God whose example and encouragement have made this book possible.

Contents

Foreword

'If this book has a message it is this,' writes Andrew Brandon, 'that the passion for God and delight in his presence are at the heart of our faith.'

This book does have such a message and the message is timely. Our current preoccupation with charismatic experiences, world evangelism, evangelical social concern or even planting churches are all to be applauded and express necessary obedience if we would be found faithful to Christ. However, if these or any necessary or essential practices and theologies are not born out of the fire of a love relationship with God it is unlikely that in the end they will account for very much in eternity. I particularly welcome Andrew's attempt to redeem the words 'piety' and 'pietism'. I have often felt—no doubt conceitedly—that I was a lone voice pleading the cause of this past evangelical movement called 'pietism'. That the pietists of the seventeenth century were full of good works is incontrovertible, they led the way in their century in salting and lighting their contemporary society. Any salt and light activists of today would find it hard to reach their height of accomplishment and success. I am sure this was because they held at the heart of their movement the same message as this book advocates.

Namely the personal necessity to fan into a great fire the desire to know God.

Our contemporary Christian scene does not seem to be producing devotional literature to the extent that some movements of the past have done. We must thank Andrew for beginning to redress this imbalance in a Christian scene which is full of so many books, and also to remind us of what we already know—that this is life eternal, to know God and Jesus Christ whom he sent (Jn 17:3). Further, we thank him for making us more aware that in the exploration of an infinite God there will always be 'much land to be possessed'.

Roger Forster
July 1990

Introduction

The traveller

The knocking was clear and insistent—rap, rap, rap! The tone of the voice that called to me was unusual; gentle but compelling, authoritative yet without the stridency and abrasiveness that one normally associates with such voices. His was the voice of the perfect story-teller, resonant and full of passion.

I tried to ignore the voice and forget the endless knocking, but they came with greater urgency. This stranger was determined. My interest was slowly being aroused.

He wanted me to become part of his team of travellers. The expedition would last indefinitely. All expenses would be paid. The only cost involved would be the cost of leaving all to follow him. He made no attempt to deceive me. This would be no comfortable package holiday or rich man's safari. The wild beasts were dangerous and the terrain unmapped. I could lose my life. Suffering and hardship were inevitable.

The risk frightened me. I tried to ignore the voice again, but he sounded inside my mind with such clarity that I could not silence him. He told me of unexplored continents, deserts and mountain ranges, islands and mysterious oceans. He said this journey would outlast the death of stars and galaxies, and in his company, I could watch the final encore of the universe and see the curtains close on the history of the entire universe.

I was silent, every muscle and nerve, every cell and molecule listening. There, beyond the end of time, I would see the birth of a new heaven and earth and look upon the face of God.

He promised me the supreme adventure.

He knew my choice before I made it. His was no pointless errand. I opened the door and welcomed him. The stranger became my closest friend.

That night we shared a meal together. Over food and fresh coffee, we talked about the journey and made our plans. He had little time to waste. All the preparations had been made. Departure could not be postponed. I must leave with him immediately.

The goodbyes were sad and difficult. To leave all loves behind for what was to be a magnificent obsession seemed irresponsible and fanatical. The clinging arms and hands that held me were almost too strong for me to break.

Following my new-found friend, I said my last goodbye, shouldered my pack, and turned away without looking back. Their voices followed me along the first painful mile of the journey and then fell silent. The adventure had begun.

Fellow travellers

In this book I draw widely from divergent approaches to spirituality, ie, Pietist, Catholic, Anabaptist, Puritan and charismatic. That I quote writers from traditions other than my own does not imply that I agree with all their teaching. In fact, I have deep reservations about many mystical/spiritual theologies. The purpose of this book, however, is not to analyse and criticise but to encourage the enjoyment of God. In the research stage of this book's development, I distributed a number of questionnaires on the devotional life. These, along with my own experience, constitute the practical basis of the book. The busy housewife is quoted alongside Arndt, Merton and the other teachers of the deeper life.

The challenge of this book has not been the research and organisation of my material, but the search for relevance. Many of the spiritual writers of the church in the Protestant, Catholic and Orthodox traditions tend to be inaccessible to the ordinary reader. The impression is conveyed that spirituality is the specialisation of a professional élite. Amateurs are unwelcome. To enjoy God requires a cowl, a clerical collar, or a doctorate in an obscure branch of theology. Such an impression is a denial of biblical Christianity. Relationship with God does not depend on IQ or professional theological training, but the desire to know and enjoy God.

Spirituality and life should be indistinguishable. The various spiritual disciplines alluded to in this book, ie, confession, worship, meditation, are not escapes from the realities of modern living but are the means by which the Christian lives his life in the world.

The revival of interest in spirituality in the West is welcome, but Kenneth Leech's warning needs to be taken seriously: 'Spirituality has been privatised, banished to the private sector of life.'[1] To a greater or lesser degree we are all victims or benefactors of our culture, and Western self-preoccupation has certainly invaded the church. A popular Christian magazine explained how God could 'increase your self-worth', impart 'more love and happiness', give 'total prosperity' and 'vibrant health', bestow 'lasting peace and happiness', 'purpose for life', and enable the individual to 'take pride in himself'.[2] The underlying assumption of this theology is extremely dangerous: God is enjoyed for what he gives. The person/God relationship can be seen purely as a means to personal fulfilment. God is reduced to a commodity like lipstick, aftershave or sedatives, purchased to improve our inner attractiveness and peace of mind. The motive for spirituality is not selfless love for God and others, but selfish love for oneself. The interior life is cultivated for profit; the consumerism of society is applied to the spirit. Such a view of spirituality turns the kingdom of heaven into a capitalist utopia.

A robust, biblical spirituality will always affect the way we live, think and act. It cannot be compartmentalised under the heading, 'The spiritual part of life'. The enjoyment of God is not a self-indulgent escape from the routines and stresses of modern living, but the impetus for all subsequent involvement in society. Paradoxically, to enjoy God involves sharing his pain for a fallen, broken world.

His love cries out in darkness.

Notes

[1] Kenneth Leech, *True Prayer* (Sheldon Press: London, 1980), p 79.
[2] *OSFO Magazine* (Osborne Foundation: Tulsa), front cover.

1

My Pilgrimage

'We need a conversion to God, not merely from sin.'

Bede Frost

The praise chart

During my childhood, frequent visits to church were a duty insisted on by my parents. To relieve the monotony of the services, my brother and I devised a number of elaborate distractions. The 'praise chart' was one of our most successful innovations. This consisted of a piece of paper divided into columns with a list of possible responses along the top of the page: 'praise the Lord', 'Hallelujah', 'glory', 'amen' groans, grunts and other noises. In an open worship service it was possible to identify the participants and put their responses in the appropriate column with initials attached. If the time of worship was inspired, the process of identification and reference became quite difficult and would involve a certain amount of collaboration, eg, 'Was that brother James who grunted, or his wife?'

Several people stand out in my memory as 'superstars' of the praise chart. There was Ivor Powell, the lyrical Welshman, who in his most inspired moments became so intoxicated with God that he appeared to be drunk with joy and glory; then there was Tom, his brother, the more reticent and melancholic of the duo, who talked to God as if he were sitting in the next chair. Tom's particular penchant was spiritual warfare. This usually quiet man could be stirred to the most ferocious invective and rebuke at the very thought of the devil and his works. A prayer of great dignity and solemnity would suddenly be punctuated by an ear-splitting yell of outrage. This war cry was Tom's speciality.

Peter Brandon, my dad, was also one of the wild men of praise. Ivor and Tom had a sort of 'spiritual adrenalin' effect upon him. A song of praise from Ivor and a war cry from Tom, and he became air-borne with the joy of the Lord. My mother, a determined and quiet woman, had been known to restrain his excess by tugging on his jacket.

The out-and-out winner of many Sunday praise marathons was a dapper, slightly portly art teacher called Mr Plowman. His repertoire of responses of both the comprehensible and incomprehensible variety was quite extraordinary. He could switch from sublime poetic praise to an unearthly medley of inarticulate noises. Groans and grunts of ecstasy, sighs and a 'yes' with an elongated vowel burst from his lips as if he were feasting on some new kind of exquisite chocolate. He was a strict teetotaller. I once sent him, via the local wine merchant, two crates of light ale. Probably he thought this practical joke was persecution for the sake of righteousness, and added to his repertoire of praise by jumping for joy.

The last in this distinguished list was Alwyn Harland. Tall, lean, with an enormous protruding jaw, and a pair of thick-rimmed spectacles, Alwyn was undoubtedly the eccentric of the worship arena. Self-effacing, with a wicked sense of humour and an ever-ready tape recorder to catch a prophecy or inspired word, he prayed to the Lord with such intimacy, humour and obvious enjoyment that we concluded he was a little mad. The problem was that he talked to God as if he were right there, and for all our looking, we could never see him.

The composite effect of these worship times and my careful tabulation of responses must have had a subconscious impact on me. It is impossible to be in the company of Spirit-intoxicated people and remain neutral. At that time I had not yet eaten at the same table and shared the same heavenly food. Now that I have, my responses have at times become as enthusiastic and abandoned as those of Messrs Plowman and Powell.

For all my mischief and dislike of church attendance, I was fortunate to be surrounded by such godly people. My parents were exemplary in conduct and were obviously besotted with God. Dad's frequent teaching on the Song of Songs seemed strangely incongruous from the lips of such a tall, athletic man. The spirituality of my parents, however, was not of the quietest variety, but more revivalistic and enthusiastic in nature. To sit here and imagine some of my parents' friends in a silent religious order is almost impossible. In fact, one of their more exuberant and joyful nights of prayer was interrupted by the local constabulary; the 'joyful noise' had kept the residents awake!

Captured by God

The absence of encounter with God in church does not indicate a childhood bereft of any spiritual awareness. On two occasions I can remember being overwhelmed by the divine majesty. On the second occasion I was no more than nine years old. The experience of God was so vivid that it stands out as one of the most memorable and significant moments of my young life.

While in bed one night, I was suddenly transfixed

by a vision of the glory of God. One moment I lay in darkness; and in the next, the place seemed to shine with radiance. The windows, the walls, the furniture, the scattered toys and books, and my brother who lay in the bed next to mine all seemed to shine with a dazzling light. Through the door between the worlds came the King of heaven. Before such beauty and irresistible love I could only bow down and worship. I woke my brother and we prayed and sang until we fell into a delighted sleep.

When I awoke in the morning, the door was shut and the King had gone. The memory of his presence remained with me, but the ecstatic joy, the clarity of perception, and that special kind of lustre that gave the mundane furniture of the room a supernatural splendour had gone. Hours earlier the night had shone with glory; but now, even with sunlight streaming through the window, heaven had receded. It was many years before the door opened again and the King returned.

By the age of eighteen I had decided that God did not exist. The visions of my childhood, I concluded, had been the creations of an imaginative mind. My commitment to atheism was not a shallow, insincere belief, but something that I held with almost passionate conviction.

My return to God began one winter's evening. Pacing backwards and forwards along the passage of my home, I wrestled with the implications of atheism. The universe seemed so vast and impersonal, a huge expanding macrocosm, a meaningless jumble of ancient worlds, dying stars and immeasurable distances. Against such an alien backdrop my significance receded. Out in that vastness there was no comforting voice, no reassuring arms, no intelligent, benevolent mind...nothing! I was alone, a tiny spark of sentient life that suddenly appeared and then vanished. Like a child who discovers that Father Christmas is a hoax, I felt a poignant sense of sadness and loss, but also acceptance.

And then the door suddenly opened and the King was with me again. Dead worlds became bright with life and creation, dying suns burst into flame and shone, huge distances were filled with the ocean of the divine presence, and the galaxies sang like huge, glittering choirs. In one shattering encounter, my atheism vanished. God had stepped out of his anonymity and confronted me.

In typical testimonies of conversion to Christ, this moment of blinding light is the moment of surrender to Jesus, but not for me. Instead, this encounter with God was the beginning of a long and painful war. I was attached to my promiscuity, my drugs and all the aspects of a hedonistic life and didn't like the idea of God intruding. He'd gatecrashed the party and spoilt my fun. A childhood spent in church and Sunday school had shown me that God was interested in monopoly, not partnership. I was relieved that there was a Creator but disturbed by the moral and ethical implications of his existence.

God surrounded me. Each move, each evasion tactic, each rationalisation, each fumbled attempt to hide from his presence was unerringly predicted and countered. The contest between Andrew Brandon and his Creator was hopelessly one-sided. Out-thought, out-manoeuvred, I didn't have one chance in a million of escaping him.

While working as a waiter in Cranfield, I began to read the Bible. Ironically, the only reason for having this small leather-bound edition of the word of God was as a hiding-place for drugs. In my naïvity, I thought the police would hardly search the Scriptures for an ounce of cannabis and LSD absorbed into a blotting paper bookmark. And even if they did, I could always claim that it was a miracle!

At Cranfield the conflict reached its climax. The Christian legacy of my childhood, the godliness of my parents, my own reading of the Bible, and the reality of God all contributed to my defeat. To have turned from the truth of God would have been a form of moral and spiritual suicide. I had no alternative but to surrender.

The wound of love

The early days of my Christian life were characterised by trauma and joy. The transition from a life of sin and self-centredness to one in which God has a monopoly is never easy. This process takes a lifetime, but in the initial stage of Christian life, the conflict can be particularly difficult. In my own case, I often felt like the victim in a cosmic tug of war. God was pulling me in one direction, while my old life was struggling to retain its hold over me. This conflict still continues today, but with less intensity. The temptation now is not to abandon the Christian life altogether, but to compromise, to settle down and neglect the quest for God. Christian living, deprived of this yearning for God and the experience of his presence, becomes an empty charade, a collection of clichés that no longer have the ring of authenticity.

If this book has a message, it is this: that the passion for God and delight in his presence are at the heart of our faith. Paul, whose writings have shaped the church for 2,000 years, summarises his ambition in one simple statement: 'That I might know him' (Phil 3:10, RSV). Frankly, I am not sure if I could make Paul's words my own without being guilty of dishonesty and exaggeration. As I examine my motives, there is still a great deal of self-seeking and an almost incurable addiction to *things*. This world gives up its grip on us only reluctantly.

In those early days of my Christian life, I had a tendency to loud and long prayers. Rejecting the cosy, fireside chat approach of many of my English peers, I decided that God would like me better if I went supersonic. This attitude was reinforced by the two Welsh brothers, Ivor and Tom Powell, already mentioned. These two men became my spiritual mentors. Their approach to prayer and spirituality was not docile. If types of spirituality can be compared to sports, Ivor and Tom were certainly not in the ultra-conservative tradition of English cricket, but were more inclined to the passion and fire of Welsh rugby. In order to show the validity of my own love for God, I attempted to surpass them in the 'noise' stakes. My prayers were shouted with great gusto and enthusiasm. If God were deaf, he would have had no problem hearing me.

This earnestness caused me a great deal of trouble. Falling in love with a French student while at college, I decided I had to put an end to my feelings. Rising at 3 am, I retired to the lecture theatre to plead with God for deliverance. My honesty was commendable, but I made one important mistake. Beneath me were the girls' dormitories, and six inches or so from my head was the air ventilation shaft. Even without the assistance of such gadgetry, my voice would have been audible to a number of students. With it, however, the effect can only be described as disastrous.

At 3 am prompt, every girl in the college was awakened by my voice booming through the air ventilation system. Between 3 am and 7.45 am, the female population of the college was given an uncensored introduction to the confessions and struggles of a trainee evangelist. Later, as I appeared for breakfast with a sense of fortitude and moral victory, my ego was quickly deflated by enraged girls.

Ever since that experience, I have never referred to the female as the 'weaker sex'. My interest in the more contemplative and quiet techniques of prayer date from that day!

Ivor Powell was an evangelist with the Counties Evangelistic Work. During the summer, he would take a caravan and small circus tent into the villages and towns of Northants to preach the good news of Jesus. A year after my conversion, I joined him for six weeks of summer evangelism. As a role model, I could not have wished for a better person. His Christlikeness, humility and love for God were exemplary. Living in close proximity to him in a shared caravan, I was able to watch him very carefully. Rather by example than by any words he spoke, Ivor encouraged me to pray and worship God.

The times of prayer Ivor and I shared together have left the most enduring impression upon me. In Ivor's company, prayer became not a tedious collection of petitions and empty phrases, but an encounter with the living God. In a very definite and practical way, God lit the fuse of my prayer-life. There were rare times during the summer when God was such a powerful reality to us both that we laughed, shouted and sang for joy. Drunkenness is the only state I can compare with this experience. The senses are so ine-briated with the presence of Christ that one can only respond with joyful praise and other demonstrative expressions of delight and awe.

That summer is long gone, but it has left its own legacy. To experience God, even in a small way, is not a safe and comfortable option. The experience of God leads to a kind of addiction; not a damaging addiction like drugs or alcohol, but something more creative and benign. Some of the more profound devotional writers of the church refer to this spiritual addiction as the 'wound of love'. God becomes more important than life itself. Without him, all is darkness and futility. To claim such an experience for myself is probably to slip into a dangerous or even triumphalist stance, but the Lord, like an angler, had driven his hook into me. He was drawing me towards him.

2

The Second Chance

'The glory of God is man fully alive, for man's
true life is the vision of God.'

St Irenaeus

Created for his pleasure

The birth of our daughter was one of the most gratify-
ing and joyful experiences of our life. Privileged to be
present at the birth, I did my best to encourage my
wife. During the final stages of labour, my vocabulary
was reduced to such expressions as 'Push, darling!',
'You're doing brilliantly, darling!', 'I love you, darling!', as I dodged a savage right cross or a left upper-
cut driven with venom from a horizontal position.
Bored by these three-word encouragements, I waited
for a brief pause between contractions and said, 'Darling, if you push well next time, I'll take you out for an
eight-course Chinese dinner!' The expletives and
push that followed the next contraction would have
launched *Discovery* into orbit, but our little daughter
was firmly stuck.

A pair of forceps was produced, almost identical in
shape and colour to our salad servers at home, and
with these the midwife pulled our child from the
womb into the light and comparative vastness of the
maternity ward.

At the sight of our daughter, my composure fled.
When the midwife placed her in my arms, I was ecsta-

tic with joy. All the love and tenderness of my father heart was directed towards that tiny human being who lay quietly in the crook of my arm. She was ours! Tiny, crumpled and dishevelled after her turbulent journey along the birth canal, she was to me the most beautiful baby in the world. For this father, it was love at first sight!

Human fatherhood is, at best, a poor reflection of the fatherhood of God. The Scriptures teach that God takes pleasure in his children (Ps 149:4). My joy in my daughter's birth is only a shadow of the ecstatic joy that God has in his children. 'Just as a father sees himself and rejoices in his child,' writes Arndt, 'so also God has his joy in men.'[1]

This delight of God in his people is expressed in a number of illustrations. God is referred to as the Father (Rom 8:15), the Bridegroom (Eph 5:21–33), the Husband (Is 54:5) and the Friend (Jn 15:15) of his people. Such titles as these express relationship and intimacy. A father delights in his children; a bridegroom delights to be intimate with his bride; a friend enjoys the companionship of friend; and a husband and wife share a closeness and confidence that is denied to others outside the family circle. In an attempt to convey his appreciation and enjoyment of his people, God raids human vocabulary and assumes the titles of those nearest and dearest to us. This element of relationship with God is one of the most distinctive aspects of Christianity.

Love: the motive of creation

The doctrine of the Trinity makes a nonsense of the idea that God created the universe because of his own need. At the heart of existence is not a solitary, lonely Deity who longs for sympathy and understanding, but one God existing in three Persons. Distinct, yet sharing the identical divine nature, the three Persons of the Godhead flow into each other, cohering in an eternal union of love and self-knowledge. All the complex patterns of human relationship—parent with child, lover with lover, friend with friend—are, at best, imperfect illustrations of this oneness.

In the words of Edward Yarnold, God is therefore 'satisfied love'. He created not from an inner compulsion but 'freely without necessity'.[2] God's intention in creation was to compose a universe which, like a symphony, would express his nature and glory. Psalm 48 encourages both animate and inanimate creation to worship God. Creation worships by fulfilling the purpose for which it was made. As I sit and type this chapter, for example, a splendid chorus of birdsong accompanies my thoughts. I pause and listen. Deep-throated calls, a sudden trilling of notes like an impromptu flute solo, high pitched whistles and the tender cooing of pigeons—all these sounds come together in an anthem of joy. The voice of creation is raised in worship to its unseen Lord.

The masterwork

Man is the crown of God's creative process. In the vivid and pictorial language of Genesis, God stoops down, takes dust and forms man. The artist steps back and admires his masterwork. One thing is missing. He draws near and breathes into man's nostrils the 'breath of life' (Gen 2:7). Adam lives! Here, from the ordinary dust of earth, has been crafted a prodigy, a being with the capacity to love and appreciate God. At the instant of his creation, man opens his eyes and looks upon the face of God. This is perfect story-telling, simple and direct, but Genesis also tells us something else about the creation and nature of man: 'Let us make man in our image, in our likeness.... So

God created man in his own image, in the image of God he created him; male and female he created them' (Gen 1:26–27).

Man's uniqueness in creation is related not only to his intelligence, creativity and linguistic skills, but also to his being 'made in the image, the likeness of God'. Walter Eichrodt, in his *Theology of the Old Testament*, attempts to show the difference and relationship between the words 'image' and 'likeness'. In the original Hebrew, 'image' was used to denote a statue or a two-dimensional drawing. If this word were retained in the account without any qualification, it would suggest that God and man share an identical physical form. The 'God' of Blake's mystical vision—a magnificent, muscular yet somewhat elderly man—would be an accurate description of the Genesis concept of God. The word 'likeness', however, in qualification of the first, is there to 'exclude the idea of an actual copy of God'.[3]

Clearly, there is some debate about the meaning of 'image and likeness' in relation to man. Eichrodt, for example, argues that the description implies man's personhood. In the creation of man, God duplicates himself. He, the infinite Person, brings into existence finite persons to love and worship him. Indeed, personhood is a crucial aspect of what it means to be made in God's image, but it does not exhaust its meaning. Included in the term is the idea of moral responsibility and conscience, and man's dominion over creation (Rom 2:1–16). To share in God's image and likeness includes sharing his moral nature and self-determination, and representing him as viceroy in his world (Gen 1:26–28). In the concept of 'image and likeness', two important roles are introduced: that of relating to God in friendship and worship, and of relating to one another and creation in a benign and caring manner. A spirituality that is obsessed with personal piety, ignoring the needs of the world, is a spirituality of escape, a dangerous flight into illusion and self-deception.

A whole man

The biblical view of man is holistic (a complete and self-contained whole). Archbishop elect George Carey warns of the danger of splitting man into 'self-contained compartments'. 'It is clear,' he continues, that 'the biblical authors wrote and spoke on the firm assumption of man's psychosomatic unity.'[4]

There has been a regrettable tendency in the church to denigrate the body, seeing it as the prison of the soul, which has led to various extremes: the repression of human sexuality, the dislike of physical forms of worship, the identification of the creative imagination with idolatry, and the view that the intellect is the enemy of the Spirit. To hold to a biblical view of creation, however, is to reject the false idea of a division between the material and the spiritual. All of God's creation is referred to as 'good'.

In the person/God encounter, the supreme talents of man are brought into operation. Intellectually he can understand and communicate with God; emotionally he can experience and reciprocate the love of God; imaginatively he can visualise the kingdom of God and convey his vision in language, picture, song and symbol; physically he can express the changing moods of his spirit in dancing, kneeling or even hoeing a line of carrots. All the varied abilities of man find their most noble and satisfying expression in the enjoyment of God.

Spiritual homesickness

Professor Donald Mackay proposes a daring theory regarding man's spiritual homesickness. Man, he suggests, is genetically programmed to respond to God. In his book *Human Science and Human Dignity* he writes:

> If it is true that God has made us for himself, then it would be hardly surprising to find something to correspond to this in the genetic instructions that determine the makeup of man. Without God, man is essentially incomplete, starved of something for which his genetic equipment prepares him.[5]

Comparing man with more simple organisms, he attempts to demonstrate that the human central nervous system and brain are more adaptable. The spider, for example, as a simple organism is genetically programmed to spin a web. The simplicity of its design precludes any adaptability. Web spinning is almost entirely the consequence of its nature.

Certainly, genetic programming is evident in human beings. Two obvious examples are the sucking reflex of a baby and the human propensity for language. The design of the brain and central nervous system is more complex, allowing for a greater flexibility in function. Inbuilt genetic instructions can either be developed by experience or modified by the human ability to adjust. 'Inbuilt functions,' writes Mackay, 'tend to atrophy if they are not exercised, so experience as well as genetic instruction is essential.'[6]

To clarify Mackay's argument further, it may be helpful to think of man as a highly sophisticated computer. Programmed by the Creator to function in a certain way, the computer has the ability to develop its program in response to experience, or to change through self-adjustment. In the latter case, the creator's program can be suspended and replaced by one of the computer's own design.

To understand man's longing for God as something inbuilt encourages a more holistic view of human nature. Man's urge Godward is not merely related to his spirit, but is the result of genetic programming. The entire psychological and physical nature of man demands relationship with God and can only find fulfilment if this is achieved.

Though no one can prove such a hypothesis, it does give a more contemporary meaning to Augustine's dictum, 'You made us for yourself, and our hearts find no peace until they rest in you.'[7] This perception of man's function and need for God has also been eloquently stated by a number of devotional writers. Richard Rolle, the lyrical English mystic, says, '...since the human soul is capable of receiving God alone, nothing less than God can fill it; which explains why lovers of earthly things are never satisfied.'[8] Francis de Sales expressed the same sentiment when he prayed, 'You have made me, O Lord, for yourself, to the end that I may eternally enjoy the immensity of your glory.'[9]

The childhood photograph

The idyll of Eden—man and woman relating to God and one another without self-will and evil—is now only a memory. Like a childhood photograph in a family album, it signifies a time of innocence and happiness that has been lost for ever. The child has grown into the evil prodigy of creation, and the Scriptures are unanimous in their witness to the banishment of man from paradise. The fall of Adam has become the collective responsibility of mankind (Rom 5:12). We have all been implicated in his disobedience. The human destiny to enjoy God has been revoked by sin. Even the pleasures of human existence are overshadowed by the obscenity of death (1 Cor 15:22).

Adam in reverse

At the depths of our wickedness and despair, the Lord Jesus, 'the last Adam' (1 Cor 15:45), invades our world. His mission is to reverse the ruin unleashed by our first ancestor (Rom 5:12–21). Translating Paul's thought for the modern reader, the theologian Alan Richardson refers to Jesus as 'Adam in reverse'.[10] Adam's disobedience, guilt and death become obedience, righteousness and life in Christ. The first man's disobedience wreaked disaster, but through Christ's obedience and death, the tragedy has been reversed; grace, acquittal and life are offered to all who believe. The tragedy of the first man has been abrogated by the Second. The Last Adam has taken upon himself the consequences of Adam's guilt, and reversed the verdict. The guilty are pardoned, grace overwhelms sin, and life triumphs over death.

Relationship with God includes identification with Christ in his death, burial and resurrection. The drama of Calvary is re-enacted in the human heart (2 Cor 5:14–15). The old life of Adam is discarded, and the Christian becomes a new creation in Christ. In the same way that a criminal removes his prison uniform when he is released from jail, the Christian leaves his old life at the cross and assumes a new identity and freedom (Rom 6:6; 13:14; Gal 2:20; Eph 4:22–24; Col 3:9; 2 Cor 5:17). The New Testament employs a cluster of metaphors to convey this idea. These include to be 'born again' (Jn 3:3), to be a 'new creation' in Christ (2 Cor 5:17), to receive 'eternal life' (1 Jn 5:11), and to put on the 'new self' (Eph 4:22–24).

The original image of God in man remains, but superimposed upon it is the image of the 'man from heaven', the Lord Jesus (1 Cor 15:48). A destiny, thwarted by disobedience, is restored to mankind: the ability to experience and enjoy God.

Man is given a second chance.

The frog and the tadpole

A tadpole had graduated from spawn. Meeting a frog shortly after his graduation ceremony, he remarked, 'I nearly didn't make it. The lake is a dangerous place for young tadpoles. A hungry pike swallowed my brother.'

The frog interrupted his soliloquy. 'Little tadpoles,' he croaked, 'will eventually die and become big frogs!'

Annoyed and strangely agitated by the frog's remark, the tadpole responded, 'You're crazy! Once a tadpole always a tadpole. To die and change from a tadpole into an ugly frog is against every known law of nature. You'll be telling me next that the lake is not the only reality, but is part of a bigger world.'

'Exactly!' said the frog good humouredly. 'And what is more, you'll experience the change and be able to move between them at will.'

Angered by such old fashioned ideas, the tadpole resorted to ridicule. 'Hop off you stupid lump of green slime,' he cried.

The frog chortled with laughter and then obligingly hopped beneath the shadow of a nearby rock.

The tadpole swam away. 'Who in their right mind would ever believe in a bigger world? There is only one reality: water!' he said, as much to reassure himself as to dismiss the frog's remark.

For several days nothing happened to shake the tadpole's confidence in his view of the lake. But one day he awoke feeling sick and uncomfortable. The change the frog predicted had begun. His slim, dark body turned green, and bulges appeared where there were none before, until he was a perfect miniature of his despised teacher.

His scientific theories shattered, and in the grip of a terrible identity crisis, he swam from the deep into the shallow. At last he came to the end of the lake. Like a garden seen through a frosted glass window, the shapes and shadows were indistinct and vague. His curiosity overcame his fear and timidity. He threw himself through that last frontier of sparkling, transparent water into a wider world of such beauty and complexity that he croaked with wonder and joy. All the submarine worlds of his dreams could not rival the splendour of this place. The white water lilies, the trees, the flowers, the hills and the huge, blue aviary of the sky full of singing birds and incredible brightness evoked awe and delight in the tiny frog.

He knew then his true identity. In dying, he had become a creature of two worlds: the dark lake of shadows and muted sound and this vast world of colour and endless variety. If he lived for ever this place would still continue to enthral and surprise him. He croaked and croaked until the sun vanished and the stars danced like fireflies on the lake.

I can find no better illustration of the wonder of our new life in Christ than this. Like the frog, the Christian has died to the old self in order to inherit new life. Made alive by the Holy Spirit, we can enjoy God (Eph 2:1). The physical world of time and space gives way before the greater glory of the eternal world. Here there are no geographical or political boundaries. A new people, a holy nation, is brought into existence whose supreme loyalty is not to the old rivalries of earth, but to the all-embracing commonwealth of heaven (Phil 3:20: 1 Pet 2:9). The beauty of this other kingdom is so great that any human comparison seems hopelessly inadequate. It is like trying to describe the subtleties of the finest French cuisine by reference to pig swill. Any comparison that there might be is lost in the utter superiority of the heavenly.

An eternity of this world's pleasure would quickly degenerate into tedium and a gnawing emptiness, but the joys of heaven can only be properly enjoyed in eternity. By their very nature, these joys are not transient but have the capacity to grow, to expand, to satisfy for ever. The preoccupation with the material toys and futile diversions of this life is the measure of our blindness. Blinded by self-will, deaf to the voice of God, and obsessed with the counterfeit riches of the world, we are oblivious to the light, the music and the boundless wealth and glory that surround us. We are like a treasure-seeker, who on finding a chest of priceless gems and diamonds, throws away the treasure and retains the chest.

The enjoyment of God can be compared to physical growth. During our childhood, our desire for God is based on our need for him and the gifts that he gives, but as we mature, the gifts become less important. We love God for himself alone. The tender words of Madame Guyon, 'Let me love you for yourself, for you are infinitely lovely,'[11] find an answering echo in our hearts. Our supreme joy is to gaze upon God's beauty, to admire and adore him, to be lost in the beauty of his face (Ps 27:4).

The danger we face today is that we can become so used to a low level of spiritual experience that we accept it as normal. Like children who are content to live on a diet of popcorn and ice cream, we can miss out on the lavish banquet of good things which God has prepared for them that love him (1 Cor 2:9). Contentment with mediocrity can drive the desire for God from our souls. It is only as we hunger and thirst for him who is both the bread and water of life that our desire for him increases. He feeds the hungry with the bread of heaven, but turns from those whose appetites are satisfied with the things of this world. The heart's cry, 'I want to want you!', should be the prayer of every earnest seeker after God. This book has been written to try to fuel this longing into a great fire.

Notes

1 Johann Arndt, *True Christianity*, in *The Classics of Western Spirituality* (SPCK: London, 1979), p 29.

2 Cheslyn Jones, Geoffrey Wainwright, Edward Yarnold (eds), *The Study of Spirituality* (SPCK: London, 1986), pp 19–20.

3 Walter Eichdrodt, *Theology of the Old Testament*, vol 2 (SCM Press: London, 1967), p 123.

4 George Carey, *I Believe in Man* (Hodder and Stoughton: London, 1977), p 29.

5 Donald Mackay, *Human Science and Human Dignity* (Hodder and Stoughton: London, 1979), p 105.

6 *Ibid*, p 104.

7 Augustine, *Confessions* (Penguin: London, 1961), p 76.

8 Richard Rolle, *The Fire of Love* (Penguin: London, 1972), p 76.

9 Francis de Sales, *Introduction to the Devout Life* (Image Books: New York, 1955), p 51.

10 Alan Richardson, *An Introduction of the Theology of the New Testament* (SCM Press: London, 1958), p 249.

11 Madame Guyon, *Experiencing the Depths of Jesus Christ* (Christian Books: Augusta, Maine, 1980), p 141.

3

The Omnipresent Clock

'Time is what we want most, but what alas, we use worst, and for which God will certainly most strictly reckon with us when time is no more.'

William Penn

They were an industrious people living in lands that had cradled civilisations and ruled the earth. Restless and inventive, they created a machine to rule the day and night. They called the machine a clock. At first it was no more than a curiosity; the ceaseless tick-tock of its voice and the slow, inevitable movement of its hands meant little to the population. Only those with special skills could read its face, but for the rest, the rising and the setting of the sun and the changing seasons of the spinning earth guided their lives and gave them purpose.

Slowly the clock that man created multiplied and filled the earth. Relentlessly its power grew until all life was governed by it. From tower, castle, school and factory, its voice rang out demanding unquestioning obedience. Only the brave or mad dared defy it.

The clock became a god of such great power that every man and woman, boy and girl was required to be manacled at the wrist and chained to it indefinitely. Only death could end the servitude.

And so this great dictator ruled. He woke the people in the morning, summoned them to work, regulated the time when they could eat and drink, discharged them from their offices, factories, and schools each evening and even controlled their leisure and entertainment. Nothing could be done without reference to the clock.

Each day the clock would sit in judgement on the people. Human value and achievement were measured by what had been accomplished in a span of seconds, minutes and hours. Offenders would be reprimanded and punished for any violation of the code of time.

The omnipresent clock imposed its image on the lands that it had conquered; but always in some unexpected corner a voice rose up in protest and spoke of eternity, the overthrow of the machine and its subordination to the rule of God.

The Western world—and increasingly the developing world—is governed by the rule of the clock. Industrialised societies require an efficient and uniform standard of measurement for time. The clock has imposed its image on society. Each day is regulated by a predictable sequence of events divided into units of hours, minutes and seconds. No part of life is exempt from the rule of the clock. The duration of the working day, coffee and dinner breaks, travel, commerce, agriculture, education and even human relationships are governed by it. If the clock ceased to function, human existence as we know it would be thrown into confusion and manic disorientation. The tiny little cogs of human life, the complex social and economic mechanics of society, and the vast intricate machinery of our civilisation would stop dead and become silent. This tiny planet has become the empire of the clock.

Our attitude towards the clock can be either creative or harmful. The clock itself is indispensable and with wise use can be of enormous benefit. Since we are creatures of routine, the clock provides the ideal way to regulate life and promote a balanced and well ordered existence.

If we are genuine in our desire to develop our relationship with God, this trend towards activism must be reversed. The clock must be subjugated to the rule of God and the priorities of Scripture. 'It is idleness not to have leisure for God,' writes Molinos in his *Spiritual Guide*. 'Indeed, this is business above all businesses.'[1]

God and time

The basic premise of a Christian view of time management is that each of us has a purpose. The election of the individual to grace is not something random. Each individual has been chosen and fashioned for a unique mission (Eph 1:4; 2:10). Our main purpose, however, is not to *work* for God but to *enjoy* him and display his glory (Eph 1:11–12; Rom 8:28–30).

Our gifts and ministries are diverse, but each of us shares this identical primary function. A proper Christian view of time management will reflect this priority. God is not an adjunct to our day, but its centre and focus. Like the hub in a bicycle wheel, all the spokes of human existence and activity are derived from this central point. If we remove the hub, the wheel will collapse into itself. For time to have coherence and purpose, God must be recognised as the Lord and centre of time. All the other legitimate activities of the day are subjugated and secondary to the worship and admiration of God. To fail here is to reduce time to a random sequence of events that has little purpose or meaning.

With its emphasis on the nobility of work and the importance of Christian service Protestantism can, at times, minimise the more private and devotional aspects of spirituality. Our heroes may be the daring activists of the church, and we may overlook people of Christlikeness and quiet spirituality. We are in danger of measuring spirituality by public success and acclaim rather than by integrity of character and simple delight in God. We would do well to ponder the words of Thomas Merton:

> Business is not the supreme virtue, and sanctity is not measured by the amount of work we accomplish. Perfection is found in the purity of our love for God and this pure love is like a delicate plant that grows best where there is plenty of time for it to mature.[2]

If our management of time is to be regulated by the priorities of Scripture, time in solitude with God is imperative (Mt 6:19–21,33).

Toothache

Time alone with God is not a legalistic duty, but springs directly from the thirst to encounter God. When we can sincerely cry, 'My soul thirsts for you...' (Ps 63:1), we will inevitably be found in secret with our divine Lover. The journey into the heart of the Son is one of infinite distance and variety. Driven on by our spiritual wanderlust, we are never satisfied until we are experiencing more of God. Symeon, writing in his *Theological Chapters*, gives eloquent expression to this reality:

> When the three personed deity dwells within the saints and is known and felt to be present, it is not the fulfilment of desire, but the cause and beginning of a much greater and fervent desire. Because from this time on, the man who enjoys the presence finds that it gives him no rest. It drives him on towards the flames of an ever deepening desire for the Godhead as if he were being consumed and devoured by fire.[3]

The Christian who through indifference has lost this thirst for God is in spiritual jeopardy. Remove the pining and yearning for God from the heart of the believer, and all that remains is an empty religiosity, a tragic masquerade, bereft of life and reality.

Theophan, the Russian saint, described the longing for God in terms of a toothache. So persistent is the nagging ache of the tooth that one is never free of it. Similarly, our longing for God should be the insistent ache that drives us heavenwards. The material and transient things of life can be enjoyed as the gifts of God (1 Tim 6:17), but they must never become 'God substitutes'. Satan's most effective weapon against the Western church is materialism. If he can introduce us to the cocaine of consumerism, the desire for God can be replaced by an altogether more dangerous addiction. Love for God and love for the world cannot coexist in the same soul.

Spiritual apathy, the opposite of thirst, is an insult to God. Rich, prosperous and powerful, the church at Laodicea was blind to its true addiction and condition. In one of the most forthright denunciations in Scripture, Christ says, 'So, because you are lukewarm—neither hot nor cold—I am about to spit you out of my mouth' (Rev 3:16). Such abrasive language would elicit a rebuke in most polite company, yet it accurately expresses God's passionate antipathy towards apathy. God reacts to lukewarmness with a searing, white-hot intensity of feeling. In his words we hear the anger and suffering of an outraged love.

A crowded solitude

Love and yearning for God are inseparable. Love can only be satisfied when it truly encounters its object. To love God involves the desire to meet with him and adore him. The ancient problem of the Laodicean church has a contemporary ring to it. The neglect of time with God can, in some cases, indicate a lukewarmness of spirit. Christ is always present when he is loved and obeyed. Banished by the indifference of the church, Jesus says, 'Here I am! I stand at the door and knock. If anyone hears my voice and opens the door, I will go in and eat with him, and he with me' (Rev 3:20). Christ calls out for intimate fellowship with his people. Exiled by apathy, he beats on the door of the human heart and requests entry. Such is the humility of the Son of God. If we are to open the door and have fellowship with him, it is imperative to so order our day that he is given the best of our time.

A rule of life

The complexity of modern living militates against solitude. The equation 'Solitude equals loneliness' is very much a modern heresy, one which has done incalculable damage to the human spirit. For the Christian, solitude should not be intimidating and lonely, but charged with the presence of Father, Son and Holy Spirit. The reluctance to be alone with God points to a serious spiritual disorder. If we claim to love God, we will want to seek him in solitude.

If our times of solitude are not to be crowded out by the incessant demands of the day, our time must be disciplined. Effective time management is the recognition of the natural rhythms of life. The existence of laws, social custom and etiquette, the duration of the working day, and even going to bed at night and waking in the morning all suggest that human beings function best when life is circumscribed by regular routines. We are not a random, undisciplined species but a highly organised race. In some traditions of spirituality, these natural rhythms and routines are given expression in a 'rule of life'. Harold Miller in his helpful little book, *Finding a Personal Rule for Life*, writes:

> Rule is a means whereby, under God, we take respons-
> ibility for the pattern of our spiritual lives.... Pattern is
> vital to all of us in our day to day living. Without it we
> would live higgledy-piggledy, disorganised and direc-
> tionless lives.... Living by Rule then, is a way of life...a
> pattern. It is like being a regular soldier rather than a
> volunteer, who only fights when he feels like it. So Rule is
> not a series of little laws—it is rather an orderly way of
> existence, which has as its opposite not liberty, but
> chaos.[4]

Whether we adopt the term 'rule of life' or react against it because of its legalistic connotation, the idea is sound and scriptural. If we are to give time to God, our lives must be regulated and organised. Our priorities, expressed in a rule of life, must be scheduled. This will involve forward planning.

The diary as a spiritual aid

A diary, a wall-planner or calendar are useful aids in finding a regular time each day for God. If we consider a time alone with God the most important priority, it can be scheduled into our diaries. For those of us who struggle to retain a regular devotional time, a date with God in the diary can make the difference between success and failure. In the same way that we would be reluctant to miss a doctor's appointment, a date with him in one's diary is definite and sacrosanct. It must be remembered, however, that there should be no guilt if the appointment is missed by five minutes or, on occasions, missed altogether. God won't be restlessly pacing before his window tapping his watch in agitation.

Be realistic about the time set aside for God. If you are a novice, don't be too ambitious. Thirty minutes to the beginner can seem an eternity, but to the seasoned disciple, an hour can seem too short a time to be with God.

Begin your devotional life by writing short periods with God into your diary, and then gradually increase the time you spend with him as your desire and experience develop.

Once we have established the habit of regular periods in solitude with God, the date in the diary is less important. Time alone with God becomes a spontaneous feature of our spiritual life. If, however, we wish to increase the time we spend with God each day, or organise additional times of prayer, ie, retreats, days of prayer, scheduling in one's diary is essential.

For those who need further help in time management through a diary, I would recommend the book *Seconds Away!* by David Cormack. Excellent instruction material is available with the time manager diary and folder system.

A time and place

Time is not the only necessity if solitude with God is to be enjoyed. Attempting to pray in a crowded room requires a power of concentration few possess. To attempt to maintain holy thoughts while little Jimmy is attempting to feed his baby sister with dog biscuits, or the latest single from a juvenile pop band is shaking the walls and foundations of your semi-detached is almost impossible. The advice of Jesus—'…go into your room, close the door' (Mt 6:6)—makes a lot of sense. Find an empty room and guard your privacy jealously. If you have children, make it clear that Daddy or Mummy should not be disturbed during their respective devotions. (See pages 47–50 about extended families.) A friend of mine, a local youth pastor, puts a notice on his door to discourage unwanted guests during his time alone with God: 'Unavailable. Please do not disturb for the next (specified time).'

Ten testing questions

Scheduling time for God not only requires a long and hard look at one's priorities, but also demands an honest assessment of one's life. A series of questions can be formulated to facilitate this process:

Questions of inclination

1 Do I find discipline difficult? Do I consider the scriptural idea of self-denial as unimportant?

2 Do I waste time on non-essentials, ie, late night movies, etc? Am I doing all in my power to seize the time for God (Eph 5:15)?

3 Is my use of time a reflection of my unconscious priorities? The delegation of time is often the index of the heart. The excuse, 'I have so little time for God,' should often be more truthfully rendered, 'Other things in my life have priority over my time with God.' It is surprising how easily we find time for a hobby, a favourite TV programme or to entertain guests. If we aim to 'seek first his kingdom' (Mt 6:33), this priority will be reflected in the way we apportion our time. William Penn, the Quaker founder of Pennsylvania, wrote these searching words: 'Time is what we want most, but alas, we use worst, and for which God will certainly most strictly reckon with us when time is no more.'[5]

If the response to these questions is negative, immediate readjustment will be required if we are to find time to be alone with God. A person who is serious about God will so discipline and order his life that time will be found for him.

Questions of performance

4   Am I perfectionist, setting myself impossible goals
     and feeling a failure when I cannot achieve them?
5   Do I find solitude difficult? If so, why?

Of the two questions in this section, I will endeavour to comment on the first one. (The second question is dealt with in Chapter 5, 'The Silence that Speaks', page 72.)

Perfectionism can only be avoided by an honest appraisal of one's strengths and weaknesses. In creating man, God did not bring into existence an all-powerful super-race. Even Jesus needed rest and relaxation. A rule of life is not intended to be a burden, but the means by which we organise our lives to give more time to God. A rule of life, therefore, is not an expression of what we feel we 'ought' or 'should' be, but the truthful recognition of our human condition. To avoid perfectionism, the rule of life is tailor-made for the needs of the individual, taking cognisance of the person's strengths and vulnerabilities. (For further ideas here, see Chapter 10.)

Questions of practicality

6   How many hours of sleep do I require to function
     happily and creatively?
7   When do I function best during the day—my
     most creative period?
8   How long can I realistically expect to spend with
     God each day?
9   When during the day can I make time for God?
     (This should reflect the importance of time with
     God over all other legitimate occupations.)
10 Are there any practical steps I can take to free time
     for God?

The first two questions in this section (6 and 7) can only be answered by experiment and observation. It is not always possible to have a time with God during one's most creative period. If this can be arranged, however, it can enrich the quality of one's relationship with him.

Regarding the amount of sleep the individual needs, Gordon MacDonald suggests putting the alarm clock on five minutes earlier each day to see how far one can realistically 'stretch'. Although this can be a useful guide, it must be remembered that sleep patterns vary depending on the pressure one is under.

Question 10 will be answered later in this chapter.

The response to these questions will determine how effective we will be in finding time for God. To obtain the benefit of these questions, it is helpful to write your responses in a notebook.

Sins and weaknesses will be exposed that require urgent remedial action; you will discover strengths, and you will be able to put aside a time during the day when you can meet with God alone. For many, this will be first thing in the morning before the day erupts into chaos and noise; for a housewife and mother, it may be the first hour in the morning after the children have gone to school; while for others, it might be an hour in the evening after the day's work is over.

In praise of alarm clocks

An alarm clock can be useful to maintain a regular time with God. This can have the dual function of summoning us to a time with God and acting as our conscience if less important things are in danger of intruding.

As a Christian, my first alarm clock was called a 'Big Ben Repeater'. It was a rather anti-social instrument, so loud that it could easily have been confused with a fire siren or burglar alarm. It not only woke me in the morning, but was so positioned that I had to climb out of bed to turn off the bell. Failure to do so would result either in perforated eardrums or a lynching from any-body occupying an adjacent bedroom. So powerful and violent was the mechanism that the Big Ben Repeater eventually shook to pieces. I regretted its passing, but friends and family were greatly relieved.

If alarm clocks were ever rewarded with a place in heaven, my Big Ben Repeater would be there, glorified and working properly. More than any other instrument or gimmick, that clock established patterns of discipline in my life, waking me for prayer like the trumpet of God.

Special needs

A young, demanding family presents unique problems for devotional life. Only as husband and wife share responsibility for the children can the difficulty be surmounted. Such sharing involves communication and joint planning. Family requirements vary and change as the children grow, so innovation and constant reappraisal are needed. Sadly, many wives who responded to the questionnaire (see the Appendix) had husbands who needed to take their chauvinism to the cross of Christ; the strict definition of male and female roles and the subsequent delegation of duties often means that the husband has his time with God while the wife is left to look after the children.

The home should not be a police state in which the husband and wife keep each other under constant spiritual surveillance. Lovingly to monitor a partner's spiritual progress, however, is conducive to the health and happiness of a marriage. To love one's partner implies a spiritual concern for his or her wellbeing; this 'concern' must not degenerate into criticism and judgementalism. Husbands and wives should do their utmost to encourage each other to a closer relationship with God. Practically, this will involve a degree of flexibility in family chores and child care. Time each week can be set aside to discuss needs and schedules so that each partner can enjoy God in solitude.

The single parent

With the increase in divorce and single parenthood, the single parent requires sensitive and imaginative pastoral care. Without the opportunity of shared responsibility between husband and wife, the single parent is often isolated and neglected. A single parent writes:

> There are two main sources of anxiety: time and money. Time alone is the sort of time I mean; time to yourself, to go shopping; time crucially, to be alone with God. All the pressures of parenthood fall uniquely on the shoulders of the single mum or dad.... Finance [is also] a source of worry. A single parent often has to work and pay for someone to care for the children out of their wages, so it would be a wonderful solution if churches could either help financially, or even better, if they could organise families to care for the children while the single parent is at work. Most of all, I wish that other Christians would recognise that baby-sitting is service. Inviting the child/ children of single parents over to play with your own, even taking them out with your own, so releasing Mum or Dad for a day, is service, especially when most of us just can't afford to pay the regular £5.00 or so babysitting fee.

The extended family

True fellowship is more than a casual handshake or hug after Sunday worship; it is sacrificial involvement with the people of God. The danger of the nuclear family is that it can become a self-contained, unfriendly and exclusive unit. Admittedly, families need privacy in order to communicate and grow together, but this must never become a pretext for selfishness and insularity. The Englishman's home may be his castle, but if he is a Christian, the battlements are undefended and the drawbridge is down. The cross calls us to a life of obedience, selflessness and service. A willing response to the call will involve the demolition of family isolationism: our privacy invaded by the needs of others. Self-preoccupation is as repugnant to God in family life as it is in the experience of the individual. The Christian family must extend to embrace the single parent and his or her children. The scriptural injunction, 'Carry each other's burdens,' is more than a nice sentiment; it is the means by which we fulfil 'the law of Christ' (Gal 6:2).

Families are not the only personnel resource that can be used to alleviate the hardships of the single parent. There are many single and married pensioners who would be delighted to be honorary grandparents to the children of the single parent and thus allow the single parent time for devotional life.

The church is not without its potential babysitters and surrogate parents and grandparents, but co-ordination and planning are required to tackle the problem. My own church is far from perfect and is weak in numbers, but the members have taken their responsibility to my wife seriously. Since I am an itinerant evangelist and Bible teacher, my ministry involves long absences from home. To enable my wife to attend services and cultivate her own relationship with God, a rota has been organised. Different members of the congregation look after our daughters so that Pauline can attend church services. A similar rota can be devised so that the single parent can be relieved of his or her children for regular periods during the week. There is nothing particularly innovative about this suggestion. The use of a babysitter is as old as the family itself. It is the context that is different.

The children are cared for so that the single parent can have time alone with God.

The church is an extended family, and as such, is responsible for the welfare of the single parent. To fail in this service is to leave a brother or sister dangerously vulnerable. The Scriptures enjoin us not to seek our own good, 'but the good of others' (1 Cor 10:24). What better way to express our Christian love than babysitting for the single parent?

Spiritual coffee breaks

During most days there are periods of unused time which can be used as 'spiritual coffee breaks'. A business appointment is cancelled, a guest is late, a job takes less time than expected to complete, and we have time on our hands. The natural tendency in such circumstances is to feel slightly lost, disorientated and restless. We may nervously twiddle our thumbs, or switch on the TV. Instead, the Christian should be an opportunist with time. The Scriptures teach that we should buy up our spare moments and turn them to God's advantage (Eph 5:16). Ruth Burrows echoes this sentiment when she writes, 'We should be misers in prayer, scraping up those flinders of time and holding them out trustfully to the Father.'[6]

The Western addiction to work can be so deeply ingrained in our minds that we have an almost irresistible compulsion to fill our unused time with worthless activities. Discipline and perseverance are required to resist this tendency to activity and bring these moments under the rule of God. Initially we may find some difficulty concentrating, but as the practice becomes habitual, the problems will diminish. These spare moments can be used for prayer, meditation, silence and other disciplines of the devotional life.

'Spiritual coffee breaks' provide unexpected punctuation marks in our daily routines: little periods of unused time that can be used to cultivate the awareness of the eternal. Seizing these moments is part of what it means to subjugate the clock to the rule of God.

Routines and habits

Without careful monitoring, the routines of the spiritual life can solidify into inflexible habits. In such a case, the cessation of one's routines can result in a rapid spiritual decline. Our faith may begin to rest in the routine rather than in a daily encounter with the living God. To suspend the routine, therefore, results in the suspension of our relationship with Christ.

This danger can be overcome in two ways: by varying our schedules; and by allowing God the freedom to impose himself upon our routines, and, if necessary, to contravene them altogether. Both solutions have a scriptural precedent.

Planned variety

In organising Israel's calendar, God acknowledged the importance of a cyclic routine of six working days and a Sabbath of rest. To avoid the danger of routine becoming inflexible and meaningless, God instituted a number of religious holidays (Lev 23). During these, the Israelites could escape the seven-day cycle and relax in the company of God.

The church can learn from the experience of Israel. A weekend retreat or a day of prayer can be organised to give variety to the devotional life. These special times with God have a profound effect on the depth and quality of the interior life. They add excitement and a sense of expectation, give the chance to stand aside from routine and acquire new perspectives, and provide the opportunity for uninterrupted fellowship with God.

It is a sad reflection on the quality of Western Christianity that we rarely attend events where the only attraction is God. All manner of sacrifices are made in order to visit a glamorous conference or celebration, but little imagination and effort are expended in finding the time to be alone with God. Entertainment can become more important than the enjoyment of God.

Unplanned variety

A rule of life is a means to an end—to establish a dynamic relationship with God—and not the end itself. To acknowledge Jesus as Lord of both our life and our time is to place ourselves at his disposal. The Scriptures are full of examples of God disrupting the routines of his servants and surprising them with new orders and opportunities. Some, like Jonah, rebelled against God, but others, like Philip the evangelist and Peter and Paul the apostles, responded positively, concurring with God's wishes (Acts 8:26–40; 10:1–48; 13:1–4, 16:6–10). A rule of life, therefore, is merely a door in time through which eternity can enter. When God confronts the person, an unpredictable element enters the relationship. One word from the Lord's lips, and all our carefully organised schedules can be bypassed or suspended: 'Many are the plans in a man's heart, but it is the Lord's purpose that prevails' (Prov 19:21).

Trivial pursuits?

Before concluding the chapter, it is important to give a word of warning. As soon as we begin to organise our lives to give quality time to God, we will become aware of the tendency to atrophy. High ideals and priorities are quickly lost in trivia. Satan will contest every spiritual advance. The telephone, unwanted guests and emergencies will be used to keep us from the most sublime occupation of enjoying God.

Trivia are Satan's most effective and deadly weapon. For many of us, life becomes so hectic that we feel like sailors in a storm. In the attempt to remain afloat, survival becomes more important than navigation. Preoccupied with the tyranny of the urgent, we may have little time to spend in the company of our Captain, the Lord Jesus. To avoid this 'trivia trap', we need to schedule specific time to re-examine our lives and priorities. All unnecessary activities must be discarded, ruthlessly cut from our lives so that God can be pre-eminent.

Time is not merely a predictable sequence of seconds, minutes and hours, but a battlefield in which God and Satan fight it out for our souls. Fortunately God is almighty; the victory over Satan has already been won at the cross, but this should not lead to complacency or triumphalism. The warning, 'Be self-controlled and alert. Your enemy the devil prowls around like a roaring lion looking for someone to devour. Resist him, standing firm in the faith' (1 Pet 5:8–9), must be taken very seriously indeed. To avoid becoming a casualty of the war, unceasing vigilance is necessary. Time recaptured for God has been won from the Enemy. Satan will launch a counter-offensive of recrimination and discouragement in order to recover territory he has lost. Be on your guard.

Recognising the human tendency to atrophy, there are certain measures we can adopt that will help us to maintain consistency: we can make ourselves accountable to an individual or a group; share our priorities and schedule with another Christian, and request a regular time when we can discuss our encouragements and difficulties (read Chapter 10, 'The Traveller and the Guide').

Do find the time for solitude—find the solitary

place, and expect to meet God. Our next chapter deals with the experience of living in God's presence all the time. Time alone with God is the prelude to living publicly in his company.

Notes

1 M. Molinos, *The Spiritual Guide* (Christian Books: Augusta, Maine, nd), p 64.

2 Thomas Merton, *Spiritual Direction and Meditation* (Anthony Clarke Books: Wheathampstead, 1975), p 69.

3 Symeon (949–1022), *The New Theologian, The Practical and Theological Chapters and the Three Theological Discourses* (Cistercian Publications: Kalamazoo, 1982), pp 34–35.

4 Harold Miller, *Finding a Personal Rule for Life* (Grove Books: Nottingham, 1984), pp 4–5.

5 Shirwood Eliot Wirt (ed), *Spiritual Awakening* (Lion: Tring, 1986), p 189.

6 Ruth Burrows, *Ascent to Love* (Darton, Longman and Todd: London, 1987), p 66.

4

Living in God's Presence

'Earth's crammed with heaven,
And every common bush afire with God;
But only he who sees takes off his shoes,
The rest sit round it and pluck blackberries.'
                                Elizabeth Barrett Browning

An Indian railway journey, especially if one is travelling on a second-class ticket, is a great adventure. There is a timeless quality to the travel. From the carriage, one can see the land in all its exotic splendour: old and new coexisting in a peaceful truce. A lazy ox-cart shares the road with a speeding bus; a mud hut thatched with straw is pigmied by a skyscraper giant.

The Indian either travels as lightly as possible, his tiny doll's-house suitcase tucked neatly beneath his seat, or is accompanied by an entourage of family, friends, domestic animals and mountains of belongings.

The process is slow. Even the trains that boast in the title 'express' make the fabled tortoise seem hasty. The miles drag interminably. Time is not measured by the constantly changing numerals of one's digital watch, but by the endless succession of stations along the line. At each stop, passengers and traders converge on the train with the fury of stampeding wildebeest. The former fighting for seats; the latter fighting for customers in what must be one of the most competitive markets on earth. The scene is a cross between a Wall Street trading floor and a rugby international: free enterprise gone mad!

A wise passenger will disembark from the train and return when the pandemonium has ceased. Meanwhile, he can relax, stretch his cramped legs, try the local brand of spiced tea, and savour a selection of regional delicacies. These usually range from the 'hot' and 'very hot' to the 'lethally hot'. Station food should not only be priced but given a fahrenheit rating!

The Christian life often reminds me of these Indian railway odysseys. The stations along the line represent those special times with God mentioned in the previous chapter. These provide the opportunity to pause, to escape from the jolting routine of the journey, and to give one's total attention to God. Such times, however, do not imply that God is absent from the journey itself. Quite the reverse! He fits as comfortably into the noisy carriage of life as he does into the solitude of the saint. In this chapter, I intend to offer some advice on living constantly in God's presence.

Enjoying God's presence is rather like standing on the bank of a great river. God's presence flows from our past into our future, but unless we acknowledge him as the God of the *now*, we will consign ourselves to a sad state of spiritual bereavement.

In popular theology, the idea of God's universal presence is described by the word 'omnipresence'. Possibly the grandest expression of this theme in the Bible can be found in Psalm 139:7–12:

Where can I go from your Spirit?
Where can I flee from your presence?
If I go up to the heavens, you are there;
if I make my bed in the depths, you are there.
If I rise on the wings of the dawn,
if I settle on the far side of the sea,

even there your hand will guide me,
your right hand will hold me fast.
If I say, 'Surely the darkness will hide me,
and the light become night around me,'
even the darkness will not be dark to you;
the night will shine like the day,
for darkness is as light to you.

The language is poetic, full of hyperbole and description, yet the message is clear: God fills the universe
with his presence. He is the God of the *now*; the God
who fills this very instant, the tiny micro-second that
eludes thought and comprehension, with the glory of
his presence.

The Scriptures distinguish between the *general*
omnipresence of God and his *special* presence. When
God promises to be with his children, as he does
throughout Scripture, he is not referring merely to the
objective reality of his existence, but to the personal
awareness of his presence.[1] Omnipresence without
the personal disclosure of God would leave the human
race in darkness and ignorance. The sun may fill the
earth with light, but if our eyes are closed in blindness, we will be unable to benefit from it. To the blind,
the splendour of the world is in perpetual darkness.
Here, fortunately, the parallel breaks down. God is
capable of turning our darkness to light and opening
our eyes so that we can appreciate his presence. The
call of Moses vividly illustrates this truth.

As Moses led his sheep across the wilderness of
Midian towards Horeb, he had no idea of what lay
before him. Forty years earlier in the court of Pharaoh,
his prospects had been outstanding. Now the yuppie
had become a nobody. His future had narrowed to one
option: the life of a wandering shepherd in the lonely
solitude of the desert, a dead end indeed for a once
ambitious and proud man! It was at this low tide in
his fortunes that he saw the bush that changed his life

and destiny. Before him in the desert was a bush that burned without being consumed by the flames. As he drew near to investigate, the angel of the Lord called to him from the bush, instructing him to remove his sandals. As he enquired about God's name, the Lord replied, 'I am who I am.... Say to the Israelites: "I AM has sent me to you" ' (Ex 3:14). Scholars have argued over the meaning of the name, but one component must surely be God's omnipresence. He floods the present with his presence.

For Moses, the wilderness of Midian and the stark silhouette of Horeb must have shone with the presence of God. The long silence had finally been broken. That one statement of disclosure, 'I AM has sent me to you', took the God of Abraham, Isaac and Jacob out of Israel's past and thrust him into the present. Yahweh was not an antiquity, but the God of the *now*. An ordinary bush and an austere desert became holy ground. Here we find no temple or shrine, a place of future pilgrimage, but an unspecified location in the stark, lunar geography of the desert. Holy ground is not a church or temple, but the place of God's presence.

To interpret this episode in crassly literal terms would result in a kind of primitive animism: God is only present in material objects, such as the bush. However, this is to misunderstand the entire meaning of the narrative. God is present everywhere in his creation, but he chooses to reveal himself to Moses in a bush. A simple illustration will demonstrate the meaning of this passage.

A host, unknown to a visitor, may share the same room. Night has fallen and the lights have purposely been left off. The room is plunged in darkness. There may be some indication of the host's presence—a nervous cough, the squeak of a floorboard, the gentle sound of breathing—but until the host switches on the lights, he will remain anonymous. In the burning bush, God merely switched on the lights for the benefit of Moses. The fragile wall that separates the temporal from the eternal was shattered. The shepherd encountered God. All the subsequent difficulties of his life were endured because 'he saw him who is invisible' (Heb 11:27). Every aspect of human existance, sanctified by God's presence, became holy ground; every tree and shrub, every rock and grain of dust blazed with a supernatural fire. God inhabited his world.

The face of God

In the Old Testament Scriptures, the immediacy of God's presence is expressed in a variety of ways. Perhaps the most dramatic is the 'face of God' (Hebrew, *panim*). The idea of 'presence' can have an unfortunate connotation. For some, it can indicate a faceless, nameless presence: unseen eyes that watch our every move; for others, the word conveys very little. It is too nebulous and vague. The face of God, as a synonym for his presence, dramatically personalises the concept. The presence is given a recognisable face; the intangible becomes concrete and accessible. Expressing abstract ideas in picture language is the genius of the Hebrew Scriptures. The monotheism may be of the most exalted character, but God remains approachable and dynamic.

The Scriptures teach that God's face beams upon us in love and approval (Num 6:25; Ps 31:16; 67:1; 119:135), and imparts delirious joy (Ps 16:11). His 'face' can also be terrible and majestic. Mountains liquify into molten rock and flow down at the sight of him (Is 64:2–3); the earth is incinerated by the holiness of his gaze (Nahum 1:5). Nothing is hidden from the face of God. Even our secret sins, recites the psalmist, are exposed in the light of his face (Ps 90:8). To describe God's presence in terms of walking in the light of his face (Ps 44:3; 89:15), or more intimately, to hide in the secret of his face (Ps 31:20), makes the reality of God's presence more meaningful. Every aspect of human existence is lived under the scrutiny of the divine gaze.

The Holy Spirit and the presence of God

The idea of God's presence is given an even more forthright and gripping context in the New Testament. Shortly before his crucifixion, Jesus informed his disciples that his departure was unavoidable. On his return to the Father, he would send the Spirit upon them. The Holy Spirit would impart the presence of the Father and the Son to all believers (Jn 14:15–27).

John Taylor, rejecting the idea of God as the 'ground of our being', prefers to describe him as the 'ground of our meeting'. The Holy Spirit, he argues, is the go-between, bringing man into intimate connection with the Father.[2] Without the Holy Spirit, we will never be fully conscious of the presence of God. With him, the omnipresent Creator will become for us 'Abba, Father' (Rom 8:15); the anonymity of God will be replaced by intimacy and rapport.

In our enthusiasm to embrace the more sensational aspects of the Spirit's ministry, we can overlook the primary reason for his coming: to impart to the believer the presence of the living Christ. In his sane and sensible book, Keep in Step with the Spirit, Jim Packer is under no misapprehensions. With typical thoroughness, he writes, 'The distinctive, constant, basic ministry of the Holy Spirit under the New Covenant...is to mediate Christ's presence to believers.' To receive the Spirit at conversion is to be seized by the presence of God 'as one is seized by a person'.[3] The initiative is God's. He steps from anonymity and reveals himself to us in the person of the Holy Spirit (Eph 2:18).

A patrol of GIs was once given responsibility for tethering a surveillance balloon to its moorings. As they were doing so, a freak gust of wind seized the balloon, lifting the GIs from the ground. Some, sensibly, let go; others held on, hoping that their combined weight would drag the balloon earthwards. Here they miscalculated both the power of the wind and the buoyancy of the balloon. By the time they had recognised their mistake, the balloon was floating away. Unable to maintain their grip on the rope, they had no alternative but to let go. Consequently, some of the GIs were injured; several were killed.

Remarkably, one man maintained his grip until he was finally rescued. When he was asked how he managed to hold on for so long, he replied, 'I tied the rope around my body and allowed the balloon to hold on to me. Why hold on when you can take a ride?' The GI made an important, if somewhat obvious, discovery. If he were to survive, the balloon would have to hold him. He was incapable of holding the rope for more than a few desperate minutes. Similarly, the Holy Spirit is responsible for maintaining us in the presence of God. He holds on to us. To attempt, in one's own strength and intelligence, to remain in God's presence, is to court disaster.

Our plight is similar to that of a prisoner locked in the darkness of his cell. Only God can unlock the door and provide light. Without his intervention, the prisoner is helpless. If, after God has opened the cell door, the prisoner refuses to move, demanding that God carry him, he will remain incarcerated indefinitely. To live constantly in the light of God's presence requires more than a passive attitude. Christ demands our obedience. The Spirit will impart God's presence to the believer, but this does not nullify human responsibility. Sin and disobedience can rob us of the enjoyment of God's presence (Eph 4:30; 1 Thess 5:19; 1 Jn 1). God initiates, but it is our responsibility to co-operate.

In the latter part of this chapter, I will offer some practical advice on maintaining fellowship with God. There is no formula, however, that can do justice to the experience. The presence of God is more intimate and personal than any human relationship. A memory of childhood comes to my mind: a blacksmith holding an iron rod in the forge's fire. After a few moments, the dull grey of the metal shone as brightly as a magnesium flare. God's presence has the quality of fire, penetrating our human nature and transforming it. Dull iron glows with an inextinguishable fire.

The artificial divide

Brother Lawrence, a Carmelite monk (1605–91), has left us one of the most simple and enduring testimonies to the presence of God. Unlike many Christian mystics, Brother Lawrence was not a scholar or a uniquely gifted writer. For much of his life he did menial work in the monastery kitchen, yet the book attributed to him, *The Practice of the Presence of God*, has become a popular and accessible classic. Brother Lawrence is supremely the mystic of the ordinary man and woman. You don't need a doctorate in theology to understand him! He devised no complicated system of theology but recognised that God was his contemporary, the God of the *now*. His attitude towards his Lord can best be summarised in the simple statement: 'All we have to do is to love and be happy in God.'[4]

Discovering the truth of God's presence, Brother Lawrence performed every task for his glory. He rejected firmly the artificial division between the sacred and the secular. Whether he was cleaning pots and pans or at work at some other practical task, he cultivated the habit of living constantly in God's presence. On occasions, when the experience of God's presence became overwhelming, 'he cried aloud, singing and dancing as vigorously as a madman'.[5] Delight in God turned the most menial of duties into an act of worship.

This big, ungainly man steps from the obscurity of his kitchen and stands before us today. He doesn't threaten us with his learning or frighten us away with an austere and ascetic brand of Christian spirituality. More by example than any power of argument or eloquence of language he shows to us that it is possible to live the God-conscious life. The secular world and our employment in it is sanctified by the presence of God.

Brother Lawrence welcomes us into his kitchen and allows us to watch him enjoying God. In the very citadel of the sacred, a Carmelite monastery, Brother Lawrence shows us that there is no division between the sacred and the secular; both are the work of God. 'We are equally bound to be one with God,' he insists, 'by what we do in times of action as by the times of prayer at a special hour.'[6]

The truth of God's presence is not an obscure religious idea. To take this truth from obscurity, blow away the dust and meditate upon it can turn every activity into a holy deed and every place into holy ground. Brother Lawrence, in all his simplicity, stumbled on a truth that transformed the mundane routines of life into a holy labour. He left no legacy of heroic deeds or great writings, nor did he found a spiritual movement. He is remembered for one thing, and one thing alone: the practice of the presence of God. This fumbling monk peers from his cluttered kitchen and points the way for us.

The glory of God must always be the heartbeat of

our existence. 'Whatever you do, whether in word or deed,' writes the apostle Paul, 'do it all in the name of the Lord Jesus, giving thanks to God the Father through him' (Col 3:17). This is the most important obligation of the Christian life. Failure here can lead to a compartmentalised Christian experience in which certain tasks are labelled 'spiritual' and others 'secular'. To exclude God from the arena of daily living can turn our spirituality into an escapist fantasy; the kingdom of God becomes the religious counterpart of the Disney Land Fun World.

An unscriptural distinction between the sacred and the secular cannot be regarded as peripheral, for the repercussions of such a distinction can be extremely serious. David Bouton, in his book *The Grease Machine*, gives a vivid account of the Lockheed bribery scandal. David Houghton, then the president, was described as 'an upright man, a devout Christian, a teetotaller, a tireless worker who cared little for personal gain'.[7] Unfortunately, he was guilty of a dual morality. His personal life was exemplary, but during his tenure with the Lockheed Corporation, he was responsible for one of the biggest bribe-giving operations in history. When the extent of his corruption was exposed, he was forced from office in disgrace. If he had applied the same ethical standards that determined his personal life to his business life, he would have avoided the tragedy.

David Houghton was seduced by a very dangerous theology: the separation of the religious and secular aspects of life. God's word should regulate the entire gamut of human activity and existence. A Christian who would never dream of misappropriating money from the offering bag can, without the slightest twinge of conscience, defraud the tax man and deliberately lie in the interests of commercial profit.

This false distinction can rightly be called heresy.

Advising slaves on proper conduct, Paul tells them to 'serve wholeheartedly, as if you were serving the Lord, not men' (Eph 6:7). A Jesus who is content to sit in church, rejecting the marketplace of life, is not the Jesus of the New Testament. God, as Creator, Sustainer and Goal of all existence, stipulates that everything should be done for his glory. His presence embraces the church, the home, the marketplace and every part of life. Dishonesty in business becomes difficult when every task is undertaken for God's glory. A Jesus who sits in the director's chair, demanding our obedience, will never tolerate those little compromises of principle. His presence and word must always regulate our behaviour. Living in his presence can be very uncomfortable.

Faith and feeling

It has been something of a cliché among Christians that we live by faith, not feelings. In fact, in some traditions of spirituality, both Catholic and Protestant, feelings are disregarded altogether. In my opinion, this view is very unbalanced. To rely solely on feelings for the assurance of God's presence is undoubtedly dangerous. But the converse—to regard feelings as a symptom of immaturity or self-deception—is equally unscriptural; if our experience is to be consistent with Scripture, the emotions must be rehabilitated. By 'feelings', I am not referring to a firework display of thrills and comforting sensations, but a deep and enduring consciousness of God's presence. This can be expressed in laughter, tears, joy, peace and songs of praise. 'The Spirit himself,' writes the apostle Paul, 'testifies with our spirit that we are God's children' (Rom 8:16). The emotions of the Christian are not suspended, but disciplined and refined by the *word* of

God. Without emotion, relationship with God would be cold and impersonal.

The tension that exists in today's church between faith and emotion is comparatively modern. It is probably the neurosis of a spiritually deficient and overly cerebral church. To drive a wedge between Scripture and experience will result in self-deception. The Scriptures are the menu that describes the good things God has prepared for his children. True faith in the word not only sits down at the table, but feasts on the banquet God has provided.

While the healthy expression of emotions should be encouraged, to navigate by them is highly dangerous. Feelings fluctuate and occasionally deceive us. Faith, like a missile homing device, fastens on to God and will not let him go. The emotions may attempt all manner of evasive action to divert us from him, but a strong faith will not be turned aside.

There will be times in our Christian pilgrimage when the feelings that accompany God's presence will be suspended. This experience has been widely documented in the writings of the church. Commonly referred to as 'darkness' or the 'dark night', it signifies a state of spiritual aridity and dryness. Fenelon refers to it as the 'night of pure faith',[8] drawing attention to the absence of any sensation of God's presence. During these times, when we seem abandoned by God, we must hold him tightly with the hands of faith. A contemporary writer who is familiar with darkness is Thomas Merton. 'Be content to remain in loneliness and isolation and dryness and anguish, waiting upon God in darkness,' he advises. 'Your inarticulate longing for him in the night of suffering will be your most eloquent prayer.'[9] Merton does not stress the importance of faith, as does Fenelon, but demonstrates that darkness enkindles a burning desire for God. God's apparent absence drives the heart into a fury of longing: 'My soul thirsts for God, for the living God' (Ps 42:2).

In some modern writings, the idea of 'darkness' has been reinterpreted. The concept is used to justify a spiritual nihilism which dismisses any kind of emotional response to God as a form of self-gratification. This masochistic brand of spirituality reinterprets the Christian life in terms of suffering, anxiety, and doubt. Admittedly, darkness is an authentic element in Christian experience, but it does not constitute the total picture. If Scripture is our final authority, our legacy is one of joy and delight in God's presence. Darkness is followed by light and glory.

The dark night experience is important for two reasons: it allows faith to triumph over feelings and intensifies longing for God. Feeling, as has already been stated, is important to our relationship with God, but one must differentiate between an addiction to sensation and the emotional elation provoked by God's presence. Bede Frost highlights the danger of a comfort-based spirituality: 'We must rid ourselves of the widespread idea that religion is meant to comfort us in the modern sense of the term, to make life easier and more pleasant, an idea totally alien to the gospel.'[10] God's presence is not the spiritual equivalent of sucking our thumb!

In the dark night, the Christian will be delivered from the teddy bear concept of God. He is our Lord and Saviour, but never our teddy bear. He can overwhelm us with the majesty of his presence, but he is reluctant to comfort us with warm emotional feelings and exciting sensations. As we walk in the darkness, we will reach out and seize the Bridegroom's hand by faith. His presence is all about us even if there is no feeling of his proximity. He shines in the darkness, but his light eludes our consciousness. The darkness enkindles our longing for God. We cry out like the bride in the Song of Songs, 'Have you seen the one my heart loves?', but, paradoxically, we acknowledge that he has never abandoned us. He is the God of the present.

Sensitivity

'Our rule should be to enjoy God in everything,' wrote Charles Simeon, the great Anglican preacher, 'and to enjoy everything in God.'[11] No division existed in his thinking between the secular and the sacred. All things can be enjoyed in God.

If we are to enjoy God's presence, we must learn to recognise his activity. A business meeting, a lesson in a difficult school, or a job on a mass production line can be the practical context of the work of God. God is dynamic, not inert. He is alive and active in his world. Jesus endorsed this truth when, responding to the criticism that he had violated the Sabbath, he said, 'My Father is always at his work to this very day, and I, too, am working' (Jn 5:17). The Pharisees had attempted to confine the activity of God within a narrow and legalistic interpretation of the Law. Jesus cut the barbed wire, kicked down the door, and released the Father from his confinement in a spurious theology. By his example, Jesus revealed the Father as one who is present and involved in his world.

The recognition of God's presence cannot be learned by formula. As God's children, we are indwelt by his Spirit. As we 'tune in' to God's frequency, our ability to discern his activity will develop. The Spirit has given us the capacity to see and encounter the kingdom of God. If our eyes are truly open, every event and incident of life will be illuminated by God's presence.

Prayer

The ability to live in God's presence and recognise his activity can be cultivated by prayer. Later in this book I will deal with the subject more extensively, but one aspect of prayer is crucial to this topic: the prayer of silence, or, as it is sometimes called, the prayer of simplicity. Recognising the presence of God by faith, we give every activity to him in silent, adoring prayer. I suspect that Brother Lawrence had this idea in mind when he referred to living in God's presence as a 'wordless and secret conversation'.[12]

Prayer is much more than a few scattered words and sentences randomly presented to God; it is the offering of one's life to him in worship and service. Such silent, wordless prayer is a 'fragrant offering and sacrifice to God' (Eph 5:2).

A young and busy mother with a demanding child writes:

Over the past year the Lord has been training me to look beyond the constraints of time (but Lord, how can I pray if she keeps putting her books on my lap every two minutes?), towards a continual, moment-by-moment relationship with him that transcends time: practice of the presence, as it is sometimes called. Of course, I am still learning, but I am sure that this is the way ahead. That inner dialogue with God, the continual reassurances and admonitions of the Spirit that can, in fact, co-exist with bed-bouncing, playing and even tears!

Every task, however menial and difficult, should be performed as an act of prayer. Brother Lawrence instructs:

We must not grow weary in doing little things for the love of God, who looks not for the greatness of the deed, but to the love. Some failure at the start should not dismay us.

Habit comes finally, and that produces the action without our thinking about it, and with wondrous joy.[13]

To turn the whole of life into an unceasing prayer requires discipline and perseverance. Each of us has activities that we enjoy, and those we heartily resent. In my case, painting and decorating fall definitely into the latter category. Five minutes with a paintbrush can reduce me to snarling irritability. The most neglected book on my loaded shelves is *The Home Handyman*.

There is no slick formula for living in God's presence; it is not an art we will learn overnight. Each action, however trivial, must be deliberately surrendered to God in prayer. Failure will undoubtedly occur, but with discipline, the practice will become gloriously liberating.

Any new skill, from riding a bicycle to driving a car, is difficult at first. But once the basic principles have been mastered, the skill will soon become as natural as breathing. Recently I visited the dental department of Guys Hospital, where an eager young student taught me how to clean my teeth properly. I was required to purchase the latest 'state-of-the-art' toothbrush and have a lesson in its use. The new brushing technique was not easy to adopt. My own defective method had become well established through years of practice. But as I persevered, the new technique became easier. Now I clean my teeth without deliberately thinking about what I'm doing. The new skill has become part of my repertoire of mouth hygiene. I practise it unconsciously.

Turning every duty into prayer is obviously more difficult than mastering a new toothbrushing technique. Nevertheless, the same principles apply. The initial hardship of offering every activity to God as a prayer will pass. Gradually, perhaps painfully, the practice will become a habit. The whole of one's life will be transformed into a continuous prayer; each moment will be lived in the presence of God.

I hope this chapter has made the truth of God's presence real to you. The God-conscious life is one of the chief joys of Christian experience. In the next chapter, we will study another important aspect of spirituality: the discipline of silence.

Notes

1 See Gen 39:2; Ex 3:12; 33:14–16; Josh 1:5–9; Deut 31:6–8; Is 43:2–5; Mt 28:20.
2 John Taylor, *The Go-Between God* (SCM Press: London, 1972), p 16.
3 Jim Packer, *Keep in Step with the Spirit* (IVP: Leicester, 1984), p 49.
4 Brother Lawrence, *The Practice of the Presence of God* (Hodder and Stoughton: London, 1987), p 25.
5 *Ibid*, p 27.
6 *Ibid*, p 29.
7 David Bouton, *The Grease Machine* (Harper and Row: New York, 1978).
8 François de Salignac de La Mothe Fenelon, *Christian Perfection* (Bethany House Publishers: Minneapolis, 1975), p 56.
9 Thomas Merton, *Spiritual Direction and Meditation* (Anthony Clarke Books: Wheathampstead, 1975), p 110.
10 Bede Frost, *Mental Prayer* (SPCK: London, 1954), p 136.
11 Charles Simeon, in *Charles Simeon of Cambridge* (Hodder and Stoughton: London, 1977), p 203.
12 Brother Lawrence, *op cit*, p 44.
13 *Ibid*, p 30.

5

The Silence That Speaks

'The word comes not to a chatterer but to him who holds his tongue.'

Dietrich Bonhoeffer

Silence

Silence either indicates the absence of communication or can be one of the most intense forms of communication. The embarrassed silences that often punctuate conversation with a stranger imply an inability to communicate, but the warm, companionable silence that exists between close friends or lovers signifies a very deep and tender form of communication. Long acquaintance has done away with the necessity for compulsive chatter. Two people can be together in silent empathy, enjoying one another's company without words.

Silence also indicates an attitude of attentiveness. During my schooldays, a teacher would demand the attention of the pupils. Any covert conversation with one's neighbour was severely reprimanded and often punished with a detention. Silence was the condition of listening and learning.

Contemplation

Silence is essential in our relationship with God for similar reasons. The silent admiration of God is referred to as *contemplation*. The Scriptures encourage us to gaze upon God and lose ourselves in the glory of his face (Ps 17:15; 27:4; 33:18; 34:5; Jn 1:29–36; Heb 3:1; 12:2). A story is told of a French peasant who in eighteenth-century Paris spent long periods sitting in his church apparently doing nothing. When challenged about his inactivity, he responded: 'I look at God; he looks at me, and we are happy together.' Great volumes have been written on the subject of contemplation, but the peasant came shrewdly to the heart of the matter. Silence draws the lover towards God with the same inevitability that a salmon migrates to the stream of its origin. To contemplate is to be fascinated and mesmerised by the beauty of the face of God, to be drawn back to the Love that created us. Stripped of all the mystical theology that surrounds the term, contemplation is the silent enjoyment of God and that mysterious and wonderful sense of being loved and accepted by him.

The desire to enter solitude and gaze upon the face of God has always been one of the most noteworthy characteristics of the great saints of history. In his devotional journal, *The Sign of Jonas*, Thomas Merton gives tender expression to this longing: 'Meanwhile, for myself, I have only one desire, and that is the desire for solitude—to disappear into God, to be submerged in his peace, to be lost in the secret of his face.'[1]

Listening

Silence is also the prerequisite for hearing God. For many of us, prayer is merely a monologue of need and insistent demands. Like a classroom full of unruly children, we are so intent on expressing our own thoughts and ideas that we have little time left to listen to God. So addicted can we be to empty chatter that even our silences are noisy. We refrain from audible speech, but immediately we do so, a cassette recorder is switched on in our minds and fills the silence with a medley of shouts, commands, and snatches of conversation. A deep, restful silence is necessary if we are to hear God speak.

Solitude and silence are most certainly connected, but solitude does not necessarily imply silence. The absence of sound indicates that there are no external distractions, but the mind can be a chaos of noise and inattention. Hobart Slade's aphorism, 'Whenever the heart is silent the voice of God sounds,' illustrates my meaning very clearly. Truly to hear God speaking involves a stillness of mind. Solitude can provide a context in which all external sounds are removed, but this does not mean that the thought-life is quiescent. The greatest battle in my own devotional life is not discipline and consistency, but wandering thoughts. No sooner do I sit down in the presence of God than my mind explodes in a shrapnel of conflicting ideas.

This experience is not peculiar to me. The majority of people who responded to my questionnaire confessed to the same struggle. Such inability to concentrate during times of prayer and silence has been documented in the devotional writings of the church. 'For whenever I try to contemplate heavenly things,' writes Thomas à Kempis, 'a flood of worldly thoughts at once pours in upon me.'[2] We are not alone in this problem. The battle to bring our thoughts into captivity to Christ and his word is universal.

Relaxation

Silence enables us to relax in the presence of God. The physical silence of solitude should be the prelude to an inner silence of spirit. The life of the Christian can be compared to a house. All the rooms of the property are occupied and full of noise and activity, but one remains empty. The Christian can retreat to this secret

room and find silence and peace in the midst of the
clamour of the house.

Silence is more than the absence of external noise; it
is serenity of the heart. Jesus exemplified this principle of inner silence. Constantly surrounded by crowds
and their compulsive needs, he retained his balance.
There was no fragmentation of his inner life, but a
perfect harmony between his private and public
worlds. There were occasions, however, when he slip-
ped away from the crowds and escaped to the desert to
be alone with his Father. Luke gives us a clear
snapshot of this practice: 'Yet the news about him
spread all the more, so that crowds of people came to
hear him and to be healed of their sicknesses. But
Jesus often withdrew to lonely places and prayed' (Lk
5:16).

This special kind of peace is Christ's legacy to his
people (Jn 14:27). Silence of spirit is cultivated in the
physical silence of solitude. 'The silence around began
to come and meet the silence in me,' wrote one woman
who discovered the power of silence in later life. 'All
of a sudden, I perceived that the silence was a presence. At the heart of silence there was he who is all
stillness, all peace, all poise.'[3]

As a car engine requires a regular supply of petrol,
the maintenance of a rich inner silence demands intervals of solitude. The Christian who is beginning to
master the art of silence will discover that he can be
still in the midst of activity. Retreating within himself,
he enters the secret room of his spirit, closes the door,
and looks tenderly and longingly upon the face of
Christ. His own silence responds to the mysterious
and ineffable silence of God: 'But the Lord is in his
holy temple; let all the earth be silent before him' (Hab
2:20).

Self-examination

In silence we are often brought face to face with ourselves. Silence is like an enchanted lake. As we sit on the shore, a figure slowly emerges from the centre of the lake and walks towards us. At first the figure is indistinct; the features, blurred by the distance, are unrecognisable. But as the figure approaches, we discover that we are looking at ourselves, the true self that has lain buried beneath the mud of our pretentions, hypocrisy and sins. A shiver of fear runs through us. Standing as close as touch, his eyes look into our own, and his arms stretch out towards us in a gesture of recognition and acceptance. At this moment, we either cry out and turn away, or else embrace that other self that we have neglected for so long.

The power of silence

Seduced by the prospect of midnight sun, unspoilt wilderness and freshwater lakes, my wife and I travelled to Finland in the summer of 1983. The most evocative memory of the country was of a vast purity of sky, lakes and forests, and a silence so pervasive that one's hearing is sensitised, detecting sounds that would otherwise remain unheard. For two people who were suffering from acute silence deprivation, Finland provided the ideal therapy.

It was eleven o'clock in the evening. The sun, no longer high in the sky, balanced delicately on the tips of the birch and pine in the western forests. The fierce intensity of heat and light which only a few hours earlier could sear the eyes with blindness, had gone. The sun revealed its more gentle face. Mellowed by the hour and draped in the splendid colours of evening, he touched the lake with a mysterious alchemy. Water turned to glass; the lake became a mirror of such immensity that sky and trees became its prisoners, captured in reflection.

Time was unimportant. I had no schedules to keep. My only appointment was with that solitary place. Allowing the silence to possess and caress me, I felt the frenzy of my soul unloose its grip and slip away. I was free at last.

At first the silence was menacing and unfriendly. Alone, without the refuge of sound, my life appeared before me: a silent movie, a succession of images that required no narration. Silence was my critic. Truthful to the point of embarrassment, it exposed the inanities of my existence.

The silence spoke. The opaque dullness of my senses was shot through with colour. The universe was suddenly transparent, as fragile as a world of cellophane. Beyond—yet intersecting tree and lake and sky like shafts of sunlight filtering through a forest—was that other kingdom. In comparison with such glory, the beauties of the land were merely shadows. The wind song, the rustle of leaves, the ache and groan of the trees, the lapping of water over the shingle shore, and the haunted bird calls gave depth to the silence and lent it a poignant quality as if the whole of nature listened. As when a person is momentarily blinded by the flash of a camera, the world about me turned dark before such light and splendour. In the silence, God smiled upon me.

The fear of silence

Surrounded by noisy children, the traffic roar from a nearby road, and the sound of the TV or stereo, the possibility of such an encounter with silence is remote for many people. The prospect of being silent for any length of time is not always attractive. When a child is disobedient, the threat of exile to the bedroom can be a highly effective deterrent. Solitude and silence are considered to be a punishment rather than a reward.

But silence is the condition for hearing the voice of God. To listen is to be silent and attentive. A.W. Tozer said it succinctly: 'There has hardly been another time in the history of the world where stillness is needed more than it is today.'[4] He rightly pointed out that 'listening is not today a part of popular religion',[5] and my research for this book sadly confirms the view. In answer to the question 'Is silence before God an important part of your time with him?', the response of those who filled in the questionnaire (shown in the Appendix) was usually negative.

Some of the most challenging and disturbing words I have ever read came from the pen of Morton Kelsey:

> An efficiently busy life, which keeps us occupied without being harried and keeps our attention entirely on interesting outer things, is probably more potentially destructive to spiritual growth than debauchery, or alcohol or hard drugs. These obvious indulgences, usually at least, lead to emptiness, and sometimes to despair, and in such times, one is dangerously vulnerable to being found by God. On the other hand, a quiet and efficient and busy life spent continuously in good works can shield an individual most effectively from any plunge into the depth where God dwells. *Time for silence is a prime requisite for finding that inner depth through meditation.*[6]

Our reckless pursuit of noise can be detrimental to spiritual growth. Even legitimate and worthwhile occupations like listening to worship and teaching cassettes and watching Christian videos can be a substitute for first-hand encounter with the voice of God. Intimidated and frightened by silence, we fill the silent spaces in our day with noise.

The fear of silence can be attributed to various causes. At the worst, our rejection of silence can indicate disobedience to God. In the silence, the voice of God becomes audible. Like Adam and Eve in the Garden, we hide from that stalking, powerful voice.

The stress associated with modern life can make silence difficult. Coiled tightly like a spring, we are unable to unwind sufficiently to benefit from silence. In those rare moments of quiet, our minds kaleidoscope and relaxation eludes us. The solitude we long for is haunted by anxieties and the incessant demands of Western life. Feverish and often unproductive activity has become a terrible malady of the soul. So deep and deadly is this sickness that it poisons our silence with strife.

Silence dispels all the trivia of human existence. Like the manual focus on a camera, silence adjusts the lens until our image is captured perfectly in the viewfinder. The distortion and blurring are gone, leaving us exposed before the light of God. In certain circumstances, to run from silence is tantamount to running from oneself.

Silence exposes the chaos of our thought-life. Our thinking can be compared to a TV soap opera in which our attention switches quickly from one scene sequence to another. The ability to concentrate on one thing for any time evades us. Our thoughts jump and dance like droplets of water scattered into scalding fat. Gathering our thoughts together and concentrating them on God can be as difficult as catching bees for a hive; to catch each bee separately is impossible, but to attract the swarm by the promise of honey is an altogether more sensible idea. So it is with silence. For our thoughts to cohere, a powerful centre of focus is required. God's sudden disclosure of himself to the human spirit can act as this agent. All the trivial and inane clamourings of our thoughts are stunned to silence and taken prisoner by the sheer majesty of God's presence. Such disclosures of God, however, are

rare and cannot form the basis of our times of silence.
How then can we find it?

The vocation of silence

Christ has shattered our deafness and given to us the
ability to hear his voice. In one of the most famous of
John's discourses, Jesus refers to himself as the Shepherd and his people as sheep. Able to distinguish his
voice from that of a stranger, the sheep obediently
follow him (Jn 10:3,27). The Scriptures are vague as to
the precise nature of God's voice. It is referred to as
thunder (2 Sam 22:14), a rushing of water (Rev 14:2), a
loud trumpet (Rev 1:10), and in striking contrast, 'a
gentle whisper' (1 Kings 19:12). The universe is articulate with the majesty of God's voice (Ps 29).

To practise the art of silence we must be convinced
that it is our vocation. In his poem, 'The Quickening
of John the Baptist', Merton eloquently expresses this
idea:

> We are exiles in the far end of solitude living as listeners,
> With hearts attending to the skies we cannot understand,
> Waiting upon the first, far drums of Christ the Con-
>   queror,
> Planted like sentinels upon the world's frontiers.[7]

Our vocation is to listen to God and carry his word
to the world. Silence will always elude us if we are
unconvinced of that vocation, and a church that
refuses to listen will forfeit its prophetic role in
society. Listening to the voice of God in the present,
we await the future shout that will herald Christ's
coming to reign on earth.

The conviction of a vocation to silence should be a
response to God. Like the father in the parable of the
prodigal son, God will always run to us when we are

willing to return to him. Sadly, however, such can be our indifference to our heavenly Father that we rarely put ourselves in a position to hear him speak.

Sitting in my lounge in the morning, I was interrupted by the chuckles and cries of our baby daughter in the adjacent room. Waking early, she was making her plea for love and attention. At this first sign of alertness, I dashed into her bedroom, picked her up, and cuddled her. God is like this. As soon as we awake and make those little noises of recognition and desire, he will gladly reveal himself to us. God is always the initiator in the relationship. He longs for that moment when we attempt to be quiet and submissive in his presence. We may not be very successful; our thoughts may scatter like buckshot from a gun, but he will always respond to that first waking of the heart, those soft cries of yearning that indicate our desire for him. Silence will unite our heart to his.

Relaxation

It is important to make ourselves comfortable if we are to benefit from silence. A bed of nails may be ideal for the world-renouncing ascetic, but is hardly the best place for relaxed contemplation of God! A firm, comfortable chair, a well ventilated room, loose and unrestricted clothing, and a relaxed posture are important. Our physical and mental state should be the equivalent of a finely tuned guitar string. If the string is taut, the fretboard will warp and the string itself will give a harsh, discordant sound. Conversely, if the string is slack, the note will be low and indistinct. Similarly, if we are tense, we will be unable to relax sufficiently to hear God and enjoy his company. If, on the other hand, we are sprawled on the sofa with our legs and head propped on soft pillows, we will either go to sleep or be unable to concentrate for any length of time. We must find through experimentation the right balance between relaxation and attentiveness. The most common practice is to sit in a straight-backed chair, breathe regularly and deeply, and open one's hands, palms up, in a gesture of receptivity. The crucial factor, however, is not how we sit or breathe, but the achievement of that state of loving attentiveness.

As I have indicated, physical silence does not necessarily imply an inner serenity. During a time of silence, the first issues are often the urgent duties of the day, ie, housework, shopping, a difficult interview, an important business meeting. These can be so obsessive that our attention can be diverted from God—unless we list them on a piece of paper, and then put the paper to one side. By this symbolic action, we are telling ourselves that these responsibilities will be fulfilled when our period in silence is over. This may not completely neutralise the problem, but it will give some relief from the compulsion of these thoughts.

The magnet

As a boy, I used to make elaborate patterns with iron filings. The filings were placed on a flat surface and a magnet was drawn across them. Attracted by the magnetic field, these shards of iron dust would organise themselves into beautiful patterns. Without the magnet, they would quickly degenerate into chaos.

If we are to achieve collectedness, our thoughts require a powerful magnet. For some, the thought of God is sufficient to quell rebellious thoughts and bring them captive. But for many of us, myself included, a more specific focus is sometimes required. Admittedly, there will be occasions when the vision of God is so overwhelming and clear that our scattered thoughts will run together and leap Godwards in delighted wonder. But on other occasions, God's face will be hidden behind a dull cloud of inattention. At such times as these, a more definite focus is needed.

Scripture

Scripture is a focus for silent contemplation. A Bible verse or a simple phrase like 'God is love' can be used to aid concentration and beat down conflicting thoughts. To help the process, it is sometimes useful to memorise the verse. The truth hidden in the words of Scripture can be God's word for us today. As we reflect on the truth that God is love, we may find ourselves at Calvary, gazing longingly on the Son of God. In his agony and sacrifice, the love of God takes on a new significance. The silence shines and becomes the silence of vision and understanding. We stand alone before the Christ and worship him. One simple phrase is the key that opens heaven for us.

Writing

Writing can impose order on our thought-life and enable us to concentrate on God. The pen and page become the focus of our attention. Sitting in God's presence like a secretary beside her boss, we attempt to hear his voice and convey his words in writing. Short, sharp sentences are preferable, allowing the mind to concentrate on God and not on the subtleties of the English language. Many of the ideas in this book began life as meditations that came to me during times of silence. I recorded them on file cards and placed them in the appropriate section of my cabinet.

Singing

Singing a hymn, chorus or psalm can be a marvellous introduction to a time of silence. There is something positive and triumphant about declaring the glory of God in song. Many of the great hymns of the church are ideal for this purpose, combining beauty of melody with sublime poetry. Hymns like 'When I Survey the Wondrous Cross' have the power to crush rebellion in the thought-life and free the heart to adore the Lord Jesus. Contemporary songs, although rarely comparable with the poetry and theology of these older masterpieces, have a spontaneity that encourages silent contemplation. The simple words of Keith Green's, 'Lord, you're beautiful. Your face is all I seek,' can be every bit as meaningful as some of the more elaborate hymns that we sing. Its very simplicity provides a window through which we can gaze on the Lord Jesus. A young man practising silence for the first time said to me afterwards that a chorus suddenly came to him as he sat in the presence of God. Quietly and reverently, he began to sing. As he sang, his scattered thoughts came together and he found himself looking worshipfully into the face of the Father.

The relationship between singing and the direct experience of God is well attested in Scripture. Elisha requests music before he can hear the voice of God and prophesy (2 Kings 3:15), and Paul associates the fullness of the Spirit with singing and making music in our hearts to God (Eph 5:18–20; Col 3:16).

For those who are not gifted musically, listening to a cassette or record of spiritual songs can fulfil the same purpose. The lyric and melody provide the focus for contemplation. As we sing or listen, our thoughts are gathered together and offered to God in worship. A silence descends upon our minds.

Repetitive prayer

A repetitive prayer can be an effective way of curbing the thought-life. For centuries, the Eastern Church has practised a method of prayer known as the 'Jesus Prayer'. Anthony Bloom refers to it as 'one of the greatest treasures of the Orthodox Church'.[8] The prayer consists of the thoughtful repetition of the sentence, 'Lord Jesus Christ, Son of God, have mercy upon me, a sinner.' The prayer has been 'marketed' to the general public almost in kit form with deep-breathing exercises included. I'm sceptical of the over-enthusiastic claims made by some of its exponents, but there can be little doubt that the prayer helps to focus the mind on God.

Two serious dangers here must be avoided. The first is to use the prayer as a mantra to lull the mind to sleep. Christian contemplation must never be confused with self-hypnosis. To suspend our rationality during prayer is certainly not a Christian idea. The second danger is to be obsessed with the Jesus Prayer to the exclusion of other methods of prayer. If we are not careful, the Jesus Prayer can retard our prayer-life, rather than develop it. The apostle Paul encourages spontaneity and variety in prayer: 'And pray in the Spirit on all occasions with all kinds of prayers and requests' (Eph 6:18). It must always be remembered that prayer is communication, not a formula.

Recognising the dangers associated with the Jesus Prayer, we can look more positively at its benefits. The prayer encapsulates the truth of the gospel. Through its use, our thoughts are inexorably attracted to Christ. As we slowly and thoughtfully repeat the words, the Holy Spirit can open our eyes to see the glory of the risen Lord. The repetition of the prayer does not imply a repetition of experiences. Each word acts as a prism, displaying a new beauty and nuance of light and colour. The prayer focuses on Jesus, employing all his royal titles in an attempt to divert our attention from earth to heaven. Jesus is the focus of the prayer. It is he who attracts, who fascinates, who calls, who welcomes, who enkindles our desire for him.

The second part of the prayer expresses our need for mercy. The prayer enthrones Jesus, but dethrones us;

exalts him to the supreme height of the universe, but cuts us down to the dust. Kneeling at the feet of the Son of God, we find our true position and vocation. Paradoxically, the prayer is one of distance, the distance between a holy God and sinful people, but also one of intimacy. He who is Son of God and Lord becomes Jesus the Saviour, the Christ, the promised King of earth. The distance is too great for man to travel unassisted. Without mercy, God is inaccessible. But down through inconceivable distances comes the Son to lift us heavenwards. At the same time he binds our flesh about him, assumes the role of a servant, and greets us in our humanity. Mercy triumphs over judgement.

We would be unwise to dismiss this ancient prayer as worthless. The prayer repetition of these words can guide us to a place of inner stillness and silence. Repeat each word slowly, savouring its meaning. On completing the prayer, pause and reflect. Let its truth sink into you, calming your thoughts and attracting them to Christ like wasps to an over-ripe plum. The Jesus Prayer should adjust our lives to the rhythm of eternity. It should calm the mad jibberish of our thoughts and bring them healing and silence.

The Jesus Prayer is certainly a useful device in centring our thoughts on God, but it is by no means unique. For the sake of variety, one can use the psalms, the Lord's Prayer or the prayers of the New Testament (Mt 6:9–18; Eph 1:15–23; Col 1:9–14; Jn 17). A dear friend of mine has made a detailed study of the Bible for one specific purpose: to reference all the promises of Scripture and place them under their appropriate headings, eg, love of God, deliverance from evil, freedom from fear, victory over Satan, etc. These he uses as prayers, repeating them thoughtfully in the style of the Jesus Prayer. Used in this way, the Scriptures have a remarkable power to discipline renegade thoughts. The word of God, according to Hebrews 4:12–13, is 'living and active', and like a double-edged sword, can cut through the resistance of our thoughts, piercing the spirit and soul of the person.

Christians in all traditions of spirituality have come to recognise the usefulness of the gift of tongues. Mentioned in the list of gifts in 1 Corinthians 12, tongues is a supernatural language given to the individual by the Holy Spirit. Usually it is unintelligible, but there have been instances when the tongue has equated to a known language. The gift is not experienced by every Christian, but its use is very common (1 Cor 12:30). Simon Tugwell says of the gift that it can allow a 'far greater involvement in all the moods of the Holy Spirit, from the most intense joy and exuberant praise, to utter silence before God, and sometimes acute agony, in union with the suffering of Christ'.[9]

The use of tongues bypasses the mind, negotiates the whirlpool of the thought-life, and lifts the spirit to God in praise or supplication. Unfortunately, the gift has become a battle line for two equally inflexible camps of churchmanship: those who denigrate the gift and deny its use today, and those who elevate it to such a height that to be without it indicates the absence of the Holy Spirit. The only appeal that we can make to pacify both parties is that the Scriptures endorse the gift but regulate its use. There is no doubt that in the experience of many intelligent and godly Christians, it is a gift that touches the secret and subliminal levels of human consciousness, quietening the spirit, and drawing the heart into the serenity of God. Tongues can be used as a prelude to a deep, restful silence.

Warfare

Immediately we attempt to listen to God, Satan will deliver such blows to our minds that our thoughts will buzz like a swarm of enraged bees. We are not alone in this experience. It is well documented in the history of the church. 'Satan's main objective,' writes Bede Frost, is 'to cloud and distract the mind'.[10] The reason for these distracting thoughts, therefore, cannot merely be attributed to the mind's response to silence. The Christian is said to be 'wrestling' with demonic powers who are intent on destroying his relationship with God (Eph 6:12). The Greek word *pale*, translated 'struggle' in the NIV, implies hand-to-hand conflict with the Enemy.

Spiritual warfare is not a modern push-button or pull-trigger war, but a nose-to-nose encounter with the devil. The battlefield is the mind. On occasions, the initial period of silence before God can involve such a vicious turmoil of thoughts and ideas that no natural explanation fits the experience. Satan is attacking the mind, attempting to disrupt our fellowship with God. Compulsive and sometimes evil thoughts ricochet into the mind. Do not be alarmed by this conflict. A simple order like 'I command you in the name of the Lord Jesus Christ to leave me alone' can alleviate the oppression, or if the attack is more specific, perhaps an accusation over a particular sin or weakness, resort to the use of Scripture as did Christ in the wilderness.

Praise can also be an effective antidote to persistent demonic attack. In song or prayer, we can celebrate the victory of the Lord Jesus over the powers of darkness. Before this battle-hymn of triumph, this shout of defiance, the devil is forced to retreat. He is unable to disturb the silence of our contemplation by stirring the mud and throwing boulders into the still water of the mind. Satan will always try to jam God's transmissions so that the words of heaven will not be heard on earth. There will be times when we win our silence by the way of war.

The voice of God

The expression 'the voice of God' conveys the idea of an audible, external voice speaking to the Christian. Such a definition can be misleading and confusing. In an attempt to illustrate how 'the voice of God' often speaks to us, I will recount a vivid dream I had when I was reflecting on this subject.

As part of a team of astronauts, I had been authorised to explore new planets with a view to future colonisation. The suspended animation, the isolation and social deprivation of the voyage had severely affected one of our number. He was showing signs of hysteria, his behaviour becoming increasingly erratic and anti-social.

Landing on a planet in a remote galaxy, we were immediately overwhelmed by a feeling of peace and harmony. We stood before our cumbersome space transporter, and gazed across a plain that stretched endlessly before us. The sky was not the blue of our home planet, but a beautiful violet, diffusing to a soft pink in higher altitudes.

As we stood and looked at this newly discovered world, we suddenly became aware of its inhabitants. Though we were unable to see them with our eyes, an image was communicated to our minds, much more detailed and vivid than any physical encounter. Unfallen and without sin, they were bereft of the elaborate emotional and psychological defence mechanisms that tend to shield our species from one another. Their presence conveyed a feeling of restfulness—an interlocking of minds in which each individual maintained his identity, but was integrated into the whole by some kind of thought transference. Guardians of the planet, they surveyed us with a benign and deliberate intent.

Under the scrutiny of a million unseen eyes, the anti-social member of our crew became agitated. He tore at one of the grass-like shrubs that covered the plain and ripped it out by the roots. Instantly the attitude of the invisible inhabitants changed towards us. We were now confronted by an implacable strength of mind that hurled us to the ground. Our colleague had violated some cardinal law of this ancient race, and their disapproval struck at us like a palpable thing.

In the dream, the direct contact of mind with mind did away with the need for language. Ideas, subtle shifts in emotion and even pictures leaped into our minds with such vividness and clarity that words were quite unnecessary.

God can communicate in external speech, but he rarely does so. Like the inhabitants of the dream planet, God speaks directly to the human spirit and mind. The impressions he gives often come with such lucidity, power and persistence that one cannot mistake his voice. The language of God, sounding in the depths of the human spirit, is decoded in a word of Scripture, a picture or vision, a prophecy, a tongue and interpretation, or an inspired idea.

Although God does speak to us today, it is important to interject a word of warning. Recognising the voice of God demands discernment and discipline. Feelings and the false voices of the unconscious mind can easily deceive us. Moreover, Satan can come to us disguised as an angel of light. The instruction, 'test the spirits to see whether they are from God' (1 Jn 4:1), was taken very seriously by the Desert Fathers. This early monastic movement was born in the austerity and solitude of the desert. Fleeing from the corruption and power of the church, the Desert Fathers attempted to rediscover a more primitive and spontaneous form of Christianity.

By modern standards, the theology and behaviour of the Desert Fathers seems eccentric and extreme, but they do have something very important to teach us. Rebels against the status quo, they longed for a more satisfying encounter with God. This of course involved an emphasis on the subjective elements of Christianity: personal relationship with God, prayer, listening to God's voice, struggles with demons and even visions. Recognising the danger of deception, they introduced safeguards.

John Cassian, an early chronicler of the movement, advised his readers to reject any thought which imposed 'a viciously heretical stamp on the precious gold of scripture'.[11] Novices were required to discuss any experience of God with a spiritual father to ascertain its validity.

With the recent emphasis on the gifts of the Spirit and direct encounter with God, the example and advice of the Desert Fathers must be taken seriously. Silence is dangerous if we do not take adequate precautions. Certainly, God desires to speak to his children, but we must never confuse his voice with a sudden idea bursting from our unconscious, wish-fulfilment or even suggestion. Moreover, hearing voices can, in some cases, indicate a severe personality disorder or even demonic influence. If we are to discover whether a thought comes from God, certain questions must be answered:

—Does the thought correspond to God's revealed will in Scripture?
—Does the thought come with consistency, or is it a sudden idea that flashes into the mind?
—Is the thought wish-fulfilment? (It is possible to

give your own thoughts and longings authority by
conferring on them the status of a word from God.)
—Does the thought glorify self or God? If it has the
former effect, it should be rejected as false.
—Has the thought been confirmed by subsequent
events?
—Has the thought been confirmed by others? (1 Cor
14:29–33)

During a period of silence, we do not suspend our
rationality. A mind imbued with Scripture is a highly
sensitive surveillance device, sifting through impressions and ideas and rejecting those that are false. If we
disengage the mind and ignore the plain teaching of
Scripture, silence becomes malevolent and dangerous.
Straying from the path of truth, we enter a land of
illusion, haunted by demons, deceitful voices and the
monsters of the unconscious mind.

Silence can easily become the casualty of a busy life.
A conspiracy of noise and incessant activity can effec-
tively keep us from the depth and stillness in which
God waits to reveal himself. The modern world is so
organised that we have little time to pause and listen.
Telephones, videos, stereos, TVs and home computers
fill those moments that would otherwise be spent in
silent contemplation. The entertainment and communication industries are in danger of robbing us of
the very quality that can restore our equilibrium—
silence! Life can speed up to such an extent that our
experience resembles a video stuck on fast forward.
One sequence of film blurs into the next in a meaningless jumble of images and eccentric movement. Stress
has become the great assassin, a killer so skilled in the
art of destruction that all are at risk, and Christians are
not immune. Each year thousands of sincere believers
are killed or incapacitated by stress-related disorders.
The peace and rest that Christ promises have eluded
us. Silence, therefore, is crucially important for each

one of us. It enables us to slow down our lives, to pause for long enough to let God speak and reveal himself.

God is never in a hurry unless he is welcoming a sinner back into the fellowship of saints. Leading his people through the wilderness to the promised land of Canaan, he allowed a three-week stroll to take forty years. He is the three-mile-an-hour God, moving at walking pace. Driving in the fast lane is often considered to be a mark of distinction and spirituality. The condition, however, for seeing and hearing God is often to slow down, to be still, to enter into a rich silence.

Put aside regular intervals each day for silence. Instead of switching on the TV, inserting another cassette into the stereo, or putting on a walkman, sit and listen. Cultivate the art of silence; make it an essential part of your devotional life. A walk with the dog, gardening, housework, and all manner of activities during the day can be opportunities for silence.

I think the times that God has spoken to me most clearly have been in times of silence [writes a young business executive], and not necessarily in quiet times. Sometimes when I go for a walk, or in the stillness after having driven the car into the garage at night, I turn off the engine and all is suddenly quiet. In times like this, I have no problem searching for words—because words are no longer necessary. I find myself communicating to God in thoughts and feelings.

This young man has learned to gather the odd moments of his day and use them for silent contemplation. Silence has become a natural and spontaneous part of his life.

For the true lover of God, silence is not empty and lonely, but resonant with the eternal language from which all human languages are derived. To enter into silence is to hear the God who spoke creation into existence; whose powerful word upholds the universe until the appointed hour of its destruction (2 Pet 3:5–7).

Silence is dangerous and fascinating. Here we enter the depths where God dwells and learn to become familiar with his voice. Christian life is no longer a tirade of need, but a dialogue with the Creator. As we listen for the voice of God, the silence speaks and becomes alive.

Notes

1 Thomas Merton, *The Sign of Jonas* (Burns and Oates: London, 1967), p 16.

2 Thomas à Kempis, *The Imitation of Christ* (Penguin: Harmondsworth, 1952), p 158.

3 Quoted by Metropolitan Anthony of Sourozh, *The Essence of Prayer* (Darton, Longman and Todd: London, 1986), p 189.

4 A.W. Tozer, *God Tells the Man Who Cares* (Christian Publications: Harrisburg, Pennsylvania, 1970), p 16.

5 A.W. Tozer, *The Pursuit of God* (Marshall, Morgan and Scott: London, 1961), p 30.

6 Morton T. Kelsey, *The Other Side of Silence* (SPCK: London, 1977), p 83.

7 Quoted in Kenneth Leech, *Spirituality and Pastoral Care* (Sheldon Press: London, 1986), p 20.

8 Metropolitan Anthony, *op cit*, p 108.

9 Cited in Kenneth Leech, *Soul Friend* (Sheldon Press: London, 1977), p 108.

10 Bede Frost, *Mental Prayer* (SPCK: London, 1954), p 139.

11 John Cassian, *Conferences* (Paulist Press: New York, 1985), pp 57, 60–80.

6

The Talking Book

'A new world will arise out of the spiritual mists
when we approach the Bible with the idea that it
is not only a book which was once spoken, but a
book which is now speaking.'

A.W. Tozer

God is articulate. The Bible is described as the word of
God, the primary means of his self-revelation to us. If
we are to become familiar with the voice of God, we
must become acquainted with the talking book, the
Bible. It is here that God's voice resounds most clearly
and reliably.

Difficulties with the word of God

Rationalism

The ability to discern God's voice in Scripture is often
determined by our attitude towards the Bible. Modern
scholarship has done us a great service in bringing to
light the oral, literary and historical background of the
biblical documents, but its influence on the spirituality of the church has not always been so helpful.
There has been a marked tendency among European
scholars to dismiss the miraculous elements of Scripture as myths. This debunking of the supernatural has
not been the result of careful exegesis, but stems
rather from the doctrinaire conclusion that miracles do

not happen. To assume, as have some theologians, that miracles are impossible because they do not fit into the frame of our rationalistic world-view, is hardly objective scholarship. The genius of the Bible is the message that God has spoken and acted in our world; the Beyond has broken into history, the Eternal has truncated time. This dynamic process of revelation reaches its culmination in the life, teaching, miracles, death and resurrection of Jesus Christ: God invading history in human form in order to reconcile the world to himself (2 Cor 5:18–21).

A purely rationalistic approach to Scripture leaves us very little in the Bible to believe. The glorious Presence who stalks its pages is reduced to a myth, the Christian equivalent of a Zeus or Odin, and his miracles are considered to be either fictitious, or else natural events explained supernaturally. For example, the feeding of the five thousand might be construed as the sudden appearance of picnic lunches, no doubt brought about by the willingness of the little boy to give his lunch to Jesus.

I am undoubtedly simplifying the problem, but my main contention holds firm: an approach to the Bible that reduces the miraculous to myth will seriously hinder the devotional reading and study of Scripture. If God's voice is to be heard clearly and consistently in the Bible, there must be a belief in its divine authorship. Our Western rationalism can banish the God of the Bible to the realm of fairy tales and mythology, but he will never remain there. Long after Western rationalism with all its associated philosophies is lost in the labyrinth of history, God will continue to speak through the Bible. This book will outlast its critics. The idea, therefore, that Scripture has been inspired by the Holy Spirit is more important than mere academic interest. To approach the Scriptures with the confidence that God has spoken by the Holy Spirit is to prepare oneself to hear the voice of God.

Those of us who adopt a more conservative view of Scripture must not be complacent. The fact that God has spoken and acted in the past is central to our orthodoxy, but we can feel threatened by a God who speaks and acts in the present. In our own way, we can be as rationalistic as our liberal and radical counterparts. We firmly believe in the miracles of the Bible, but do not expect God to act and speak in a similar way today. Our theology can exile God to a time warp. All miracles, we argue, were suspended after the first century AD and will only resume when Christ returns to earth. During the interregnum we should be content with the Bible alone. In its most extreme form, this approach can lead to bibliolatry—the worship of the Bible rather than of God. The Scriptures must never be a 'God substitute', but the means by which we encounter him and become acquainted with his voice.

The Scriptures constitute a series of clearly marked signposts that point us to God. If we confuse the signposts with the destination, we will soon equate an academic knowledge of Scripture with personal relationship with God. To possess the truth without knowing God is rather like receiving love letters from one's wife without consumating the relationship or living together in intimacy. The Bible is relevant because its author is present and dynamic in our world. The very same God whose words and actions are recorded in the Bible longs to speak to us through its writings today. The economics, the warfare, the methods of transportation, the science, the politics and the culture of the Bible are totally unlike our own, yet God speaks through its antiquity with a contemporary voice.

Familiarity

Any book, however subtle the plot or brilliant the prose, will become boring and irrelevant if it is read repeatedly. The Bible is no exception. At the risk of serious reprisals, I will come out of the closet. There are occasions when, reading a familiar passage of Scripture, I find my attention wandering. The Scriptures are not to blame for my inattention, but rather my attitude towards them. If we are to hear God speaking in the Bible, we must reorientate our thinking. It is not sufficient to believe in the uniqueness and reliability of the word of God; there must also be the conviction that we will hear the whisper of the living Word in his written word. Such a conviction will help us to overcome the problem of familiarity. Even a passage of Scripture that we have read many times can assume a new significance when God speaks.

Novelty

The love of novelty and sensation is one of the characteristics of Western society. The free world prides itself in defending the rights of the individual, yet perpetuates one of the most subtle and effective forms of totalitarianism in history.

Orwell's *Nineteen Eighty-four* is a chillingly prophetic novel. It describes a society ruled by Big Brother, a semi-mythical figure who controls the minds and affections of the people through the Ministry of Truth, an evil propaganda machine. The misinformation and lies of this agency are referred to as 'Newspeak', a style of mind control that involves the corruption of language. So effective is this method that lies are accepted as truth and hatred as love. All the unique aspects of the human spirit—beauty, love, creativity and freedom—are regarded as subversive. God's world is recreated in the image of a demonic state.

With the demise of communism, Big Brother has been discredited, but not for long. Without our being aware of it, he has been resurrected in a new disguise. Through an almost total domination of the mass media, Big Brother continues to disseminate his propaganda. The message and approach are very different, but he achieves the same end: the total control of the public mind. The vastly expensive advertising programmes that have accompanied the consumer revolution are a modern example of 'Newspeak'. Few of the claims that are made can be properly verified, and some are deliberately misleading. Truth is sacrificed in the interests of profitability. Our insecurities, weaknesses and longings are ruthlessly and cleverly exploited by big business.

This new form of totalitarianism has achieved the impossible: the manipulation of entire populations without their being aware of it. Our hands are not manacled—we still maintain the illusion of freedom—but our minds have been taken captive by the idea that the meaning of life is found in the accumulation of possessions. Man becomes a voracious consumer, only satisfied when he is gorged on some new gadget or experience. In fact, Western materialism has proved far more effective in stifling the spiritual life than the ideological materialism of communism.

Tragically, this Western love of novelty and sensation can influence our attitude to the Scriptures. More exciting examples of God's speaking, eg, tongues, prophecy, and angelic visitation, are sometimes preferred to Bible reading, meditation and study. We are all susceptible to this temptation. Paul's letter to the Corinthians tells us not to despise spiritual gifts, but it also warns of the consequences of an overemphasis on the gifts of the Spirit. The word of God will always remain the primary means of his self-revelation to us.

If we are to grow strong in God and discern his voice, we must pay careful heed to the Bible.

Encouraging his protégé Timothy to be diligent in Bible study, Paul draws attention to its supernatural origin: 'All Scripture is God-breathed and is useful for teaching, rebuking, correcting and training in righteousness' (2 Tim 3:16). The unusual expression 'God-breathed' translates the Greek adjective *theopneustos*, identifying the formation and inspiration of Scripture with the activity of the Holy Spirit. This emphasis is not unique to Paul; Peter, writing in his second Epistle, states that prophecy was not given at the behest of man, but the prophets 'spoke from God as they were carried along by the Holy Spirit' (2 Pet 1:21). Jesus, too, attributes the creation of Scripture to the Holy Spirit (Mk 12:36). The same Holy Spirit who inspired the Bible interprets its message to us today.

The Bible, therefore, is not dead or inert, the memoirs of a God who has withdrawn into obscurity and perpetual silence, but 'living and active' (Heb 4:12). To unravel its message and hear the voice of God requires a multi-disciplinary approach. No one method, eg, meditation, will unstop our ears and make God's voice audible to his people. Each approach to Scripture is so closely related that to adopt one in isolation will invariably mute the voice of God. Accordingly, I will detail the various approaches to the Bible and endeavour to show their relationship.

Reading the Bible

If we are to read the Bible naturally, it is better to have a modern version. The language of the King James Version is sublime in its poetry, but for most people its archaic phrasing makes understanding difficult. God is our contemporary. He desires to speak to us in language that we can understand, not in the vernacular of a bygone age. For most of us language such as 'verily', 'bowels of compassion', 'bloweth', 'thou', 'thee', 'doest' and 'mightest' distances God from us. Understanding Scripture is difficult enough without having to struggle with the nuances of seventeenth-century English.

Silence

Before beginning to read the Scriptures, sit in silence for a minute. (See also Chapter 5, 'The Silence that Speaks'.)

Dependence

As has already been shown, the Holy Spirit is responsible for the inspiration of Scripture. Only as we learn to depend on him for enlightenment will God speak. Thomas à Kempis recognised his dependence on the Spirit if he were to hear God speak in Scripture: 'The prophets can preach your word, but they cannot bestow the Spirit. They speak most eloquently, but if you are silent, they cannot fire the heart. They instruct in the letter, but they cannot open the understanding.'[1]

Expectancy

Expect God to speak as you read his word. One of the most evocative portraits of Christ in Scripture is found in Revelation 3:20: 'Here I am! I stand at the door and knock. If anyone hears my voice and opens the door, I will go in and eat with him, and he with me.' Our capacity to hear the voice of God can be dulled by familiarity. Christ can call out to us and knock upon our hearts in longing for intimacy, but so deep is our apathy that we are oblivious to him.

The Bible describes God and the believer as lovers. That unique quality of expectation that lovers feel at the prospect of intimacy should characterise our approach to God and Scripture. The longing of the child of God is never disappointed. The heart that cries 'I long to hear your voice, O God!' will be satisfied with the food and drink of his living word.

Reflection

There is no special reward for those who race through the Scriptures as if they were driving in a Grand Prix. The Christian who reads a chapter prayerfully and reflectively will probably derive more benefit from the exercise than his speeding counterpart. It is not the length of the Bible reading that is important, but the quality of one's understanding and application. To attempt to speed read the Bible can be as potentially damaging as eating too rapidly; undigested food is of little value.

In order to digest the word of God properly, we must read prayerfully and reflectively. Madame Guyon expressed the importance of this very clearly:

> If you read quickly it will benefit you little. You will be like a bee that merely skims the surface of the flower. Instead, in this new way of reading with prayer, you must become as the bee who penetrates deeply into the flower. You plunge deeper within to remove its nectar.[2]

This approach to Scripture has been aptly described as 'spiritual reading'. Christopher Bryant says of this discipline, 'The growth of faith is fostered by spiritual reading. This is not the rapid reading with which a person reads a newspaper or novel, but slow, reflective prayerful reading of Scripture. It is a reading designed to awaken Godward aspirations.'[3] In spiritual reading, each word is relished and enjoyed. The Bible is not a junk food menu but a cuisine of delicious subtlety and variety. To gorge the meal in fast, greedy mouthfuls is to deprive oneself of a remarkable blend of tastes and exotic flavours. The word of God needs to be carefully chewed, tasted and savoured so that each morsel yields its delights. God is a master chef. If we are to do justice to the banquet of his word, unhurried feasting is imperative.

Obedience

The regularity with which we hear God speaking is often determined by our willingness to obey him. Hearing God is not an exercise in pious self-indulgence, but something altogether more demanding and dangerous. When God speaks, he demands obedience.

There is an unfortunate tendency to view spirituality in terms of self-gratification. This heresy can turn the Creator into a harmless chattel. Like the traditional English butler, he stands unobtrusively at our shoulder ready to turn every whim into a reality. This nervous, ingratiating God is much too polite ever to mention obedience. Our will is his command. This inability to take obedience seriously can result in a silent Bible. Only as we diligently obey the voice of God will his voice continue to resound in Scripture.

Concentration

Even with the correct approach to Bible reading our attention can still wander. One effective antidote is to keep a spiritual journal. As we read the Scriptures we can write our discoveries in the journal. This has a threefold effect: it concentrates the mind, enables one to recall and remember the reading, and provides a written account of the spiritual pilgrimage. Some of the greatest classics of Christian literature have been such journals. They provide deep insight into the struggles, temptations, joys and personal lives of their authors. An inspiring contemporary example is the journal of the missionary martyr Jim Elliot.

Colour coding is yet another concentration aid. Various topics, eg, prayer, covenant, justice, mercy, can be coded in colour. Each time a chosen theme appears in Scripture we highlight it in the appropriate colour. The advantage of this method is that it allows us to follow a selection of subjects from Genesis to Revelation. There is, however, at least one problem with this approach: the Christian's Bible will eventually become overcoloured and need replacement.

The most simple and obvious way of riveting attention on Scripture is to read aloud. A mind that quickly degenerates into a jumble of untidy thoughts can be brought under control by the simple expedient of speaking aloud. Interestingly, the most common Hebrew verb translated 'to meditate' (hagah) denotes audible speech.[4] The Old Testament and rabbinical idea of meditation, therefore, 'is an exercising of memory based on the repetition of words and phrases pronounced aloud'.[5] To read the Scriptures aloud does indeed encourage concentration and memorisation of the word of God.

Biblical meditation

Biblical meditation is important if we are to delve deeply into the word of God. Reading the Scriptures can be compared to a slow hike through rapidly changing terrain. Mountains, deserts, rolling hills and grasslands follow each other in glorious succession. At times the road is arduous and dangerous, but sometimes it can provide vistas of such originality and beauty that one is left breathless and dazed. Meditation, however, is a pause in the trek, an opportunity to stop and admire the scenery more closely. Detail that would otherwise have eluded observation can be carefully examined through binoculars. In meditation, the spectator and his object are brought together in a relationship of rapt concentration and mutual inter-change. As the Christian meditates on the word and becomes immersed in its message, God begins to illuminate and speak.

Meditation is a lost art among Christians. In some groups, the word itself has assumed a negative con-notation. For many Christians, 'meditation' smacks of a dangerous Eastern practice. For the Eastern guru, to meditate is to search inwards for enlightenment; to lose one's ego and personal identity in a timeless pool of consciousness. In this context, meditation demands passivity of mind and the suspension of the cognitive process. But Christian meditation is of a different order altogether. One of the most comprehensive defi-nitions can be found in Jim Packer's excellent book, *Knowing God*:

> Meditation is the activity of calling to mind, and thinking over, and dwelling on, and applying to oneself, the various things that one knows about the works and ways and purpose and promises of God. It is an activity of holy thought, consciously performed in the presence of God, under the eye of God, by the help of God, as a means of communion with God. Its purpose is to clear one's mental and spiritual vision of God, and let his truth make its proper impact on one's mind and heart.[6]

Writing in the *Dictionary of Spirituality*, Jean Leclercq uses the metaphor of digestion to express the meaning of meditation, commenting that 'the text is chewed and ruminated in order to get out of it the whole savour, the whole taste of the sweetness of God'.[7]

It should be clear from these definitions that Chris-tian meditation is not the negation of the mind. The intellect, disciplined and illuminated by the Spirit, is of crucial importance in the exercise, but this does not

imply that Christian meditation is merely the application of logic to God and his word. To engage in meditation is to bring all our talents of rationality,
intuition, imagination, feeling and volition into play.

One can meditate upon God (Ps 63:6), an attribute
of God (Ps 48:9), the Scriptures (Ps 1:2; 119:15–23), the
works of God (Ps 77:12), and creation (Ps 8:3). This list
of material is by no means exhaustive, for all human
experience and activity can provide fuel for Spirit-
inspired meditation.

How to meditate on Scripture

Meditation should arise naturally out of our reading of
Scripture, and a suggested approach follows:

—Pray that God will give illumination and speak
through his word.
—Read the verse or passage slowly and reflectively,
relishing each word and subtle nuance of meaning.
—Engage the mind in a dialogue with Scripture.
Attempt to grapple with its meaning and message.
—Cultivate the intuition. Perception is as much part
of meditation as are the more logical and conscious
patterns of thought. A sudden intuition can cast
light on a Scripture and prise from the text a meaning that has eluded rational thought and examination.
—Do not repress emotions. Meditation is not a form
of emotional detachment. To meditate upon Scripture is to vivify human feelings. For example, if we
meditate on the healing of the paralysed man in
Mark 2:1–12, we share the man's suffering in his
paralysis, feel his embarrassment as he is lowered
through the roof, sense the dawning of hope as he
confronts Christ, and almost explode with joy when
he is forgiven and healed.
—Use your imagination. If you are meditating on a

story or parable, employ your creative gifts and try to visualise it. St Francis de Sales offers some useful advice on imagination in his *Introduction to the Devout Life*:

> If you wish to meditate on our Lord on the Cross, imagine that you are on Mount Calvary, and that you behold and hear all that was done or said on the day of passion. Or, if you prefer it, for it is all one, imagine that in the very place where you are they are crucifying our Lord in the manner described by the holy evangelists.[8]

Ignatius Loyola recommends sensuous involvement in Scripture. In his *Spiritual Exercises*, he suggests that as we meditate on an event in the life of Christ, the five senses, ie, sight, hearing, smell, taste and touch, should be awakened and involved. There is nothing particularly dangerous in this approach, but we must guard against fantasy. If the imagination is not to become renegade, it must be subdued and disciplined by Scripture. An undisciplined imagination can turn meditation into makebelieve. The truth of God becomes a pious fairy story full of delightful fantasies.

Again, record your meditation in a notebook or journal. Writing aids concentration and helps to prevent daydreaming.

Meditation and action

The purpose of meditation is not to fill our heads and hearts with spiritual fantasies and ecstatic feelings, but to prompt us to love and obey God. Unlike the reading of Scripture, meditation can be practised anywhere. A walk to the supermarket or local shops, gardening, housework, cleaning the car and all manner of activities that do not require serious thought can be used for meditation. The psalmist's description of the righteous man as one who meditates day and night (Ps 1:2) is not as far-fetched as it may first appear. By memorising verses and passages of Scripture, we can recall them to mind whenever opportunity occurs. I know of one busy housewife who stuck scriptures all over her kitchen walls to encourage meditation. It didn't do much for the decor of the kitchen, but it enabled her to use every spare moment in prayer and reflection on the word of God. For her, meditation was not a complicated spiritual discipline but a way of life—one that leads to and through obedience.

Study

There can be some truth in the criticism that evangelical faith is simplistic, slogan-ridden and 'other worldly'. Singing our triumphalistic songs about the reign and victory of God, we fall strangely silent when confronted with the lethal missile silos that could write the epitaph of our world. What does the reign of God mean to the starving children of famine, the oppressed victim of racism, brave men and women who have been shot, tortured and imprisoned for nothing more sinister than the dream of freedom? Where is the reign of God in all this anarchy and injustice? Only as we struggle with the word will we begin to discern the voice of God and hear him addressing the issues of our time. If we are to let Scripture speak today there can be no alternative to serious, prayerful study. Such a painful and costly interaction with Scripture will result in an authentically prophetic approach to society.

The word 'study' has an unfortunate connotation. For the person who has found Western education stifling and unstimulating, 'study' may be off-putting. For others, study may have been an important part of life for a number of years; perhaps they relate better to the printed page than to people; concepts and ideas are more important than their practical outworking.

Whatever our background and capabilities, Bible study is important if we are to hear the voice of God. For those who remain unconvinced, let me argue from daily life. Study is something we all engage in, albeit unconsciously. Scrutinising a bus timetable, referring to a recipe in a cookery book, examining a car manual to change a gearbox, reading the instructions included with a food processor—all can rightly be called studying. We absorb information so that we can take practical action. Even if we dislike academic work, we should not avoid Bible study. It is as much a part of Christian life as eating, drinking and sleeping. The measure of sophistication that one brings to study will depend upon intelligence, aptitude and experience, but there is no way that we can avoid the discipline if we desire to hear the voice of God.

Part of the struggle and challenge of study is the ability to take difficult concepts and express them in practical experience. The engineering expertise to understand the complexities of car design is of little value if the mechanic has no skill with a spanner. Similarly, the purpose of study is not to make us champions at *Mastermind*, but to discern God's voice and obey him. To study in isolation from life is dangerous. Truth becomes irresistible when it duplicates itself in the life of the Christian. Study, therefore, is a practical process whereby we unravel the word of God *in order to practise it*.

Mind and spirit dualism

One reason why some Christians have been discouraged from study is the distrust of the intellect. Serious thought may even be considered inimical to spirituality and relationship with God. If God is to be experienced, some argue, the intellect must be

silenced. Such a view is extremely dangerous. The
Bible demonstrates a healthy respect for the mind,
referring to it as being renewed (Eph 4:23), and showing its importance in the process of revelation (1 Cor
14:13–17).

Mind and spirit functioning together are integral to
the human capacity to understand God. Some disciplines such as contemplation involve a more relaxed
attitude towards listening to God; but study, as noted
above, involves struggle and conflict. All the student's
powers of intellect and concentration are involved in
the task of study and elucidation. As the study of the
book or theme develops, the whisper of God becomes
a great shout.

According to popular mythology, Martin Luther
received his revelation of justification by faith as he
crawled up the twenty-eight steps of the Scala Sancta
in Rome. In fact this is an apocryphal account of the
great Reformer's enlightenment. As a doctor of theology and a popular preacher, Luther struggled to an
understanding of justification by faith. Enlightenment, when it came, was not the sudden intuition of a
moment, but the consequence of extensive study and
reflection.

The medieval view that the soul could be united to
God by a difficult ascent from carnality to spiritual
perfection did not correspond with Luther's experience. As he looked into the depths of his own heart, he
saw only darkness and sin. Union with God was
impossible because of his moral antipathy towards
him. Desperate yet determined, Luther turned to
Scripture and the writings of the Church Fathers for
solace.

Slowly and painfully the doctrine that was to shake
Christendom and bring about the Protestant Reforma-
tion took shape in his mind. Diligent and daring study
was the means by which Luther heard the voice of

God. This difficult and traumatic labour gave birth to a new understanding of justification by faith. Here was no passive or detached labour, but one of soul agony, blood and tears. God could easily have sent an angel to teach Luther the truth, or given him a prophecy or revelation, but instead he chose the more costly medium of study and disciplined thought.

Study of the Bible should not be a dull, cerebral affair, but a dialogue with the living Word himself. We reach beyond the words of Scripture to the divine Author. Study awakens the mind and allows the Holy Spirit to discipline and illuminate our intellects. The study of Scripture should include doctrine, ethics, the books of the Bible and church history. It is outside the scope of this book to give detailed information on study techniques and study guides, but a few suggestions follow.

Organisation

Study requires careful organisation and a consideration of practical issues:

—Choose a subject thoughtfully before commencing the study.
—Organise a time each week for study. If you haven't studied for a number of years, do not be too ambitious. Thirty minutes to an hour each week is sufficient for the beginner.
—Obtain basic books that will help you in your Bible study. A Bible dictionary and commentary, a concordance, a word book giving the meaning of Greek and Hebrew vocabulary, a Bible atlas and a modern translation of the Bible should be sufficient to begin with. The depth of approach will increase with knowledge and practice.
—Develop a reliable filing system. Quotations and illustrations that arise from your study can be stored in a home computer or file card cabinet.

—A notebook and pen are indispensable. Writing notes enables the student to express and decode difficult concepts. Moreover, writing aids the memory and provides documentation of study.

—Seek a mentor. A person experienced in the study of the Bible can provide helpful advice and suggestions. (See Chapter 10.)

Method of study

Having organised your study time, you are ready to begin. If you are studying a Bible book, decide on the particular passage you wish to study. Read this carefully and meditate upon it.

Write a summary of the passage, making sure that you include original insights in your notes. When you are satisfied that you have extracted all the gold dust from the sieve of Scripture, turn to your books. Isolate key words and discover their meaning in the original language. Read your commentary carefully and include extra information in your notes. For further clarification, consult a Bible dictionary or atlas.

During a period of study of over an hour, pause every twenty minutes or so and reread your notes, attempting to commit key data to memory. Tony Buzan, in his intriguing little book, *Use Your Head*, wrote, 'One of the most significant aspects of proper review is the accumulative effect it has on learning, thinking and remembering. The person who does not review is continually wasting the effort he puts into a learning task.'[9]

At the conclusion of the study time, list the things you have learned and commit them to memory. If there are any specific instructions, eg, 'Do not judge, or you too will be judged' (Mt 7:1), think carefully how these can be implemented. *Academic study* enables the student to obtain knowledge; *devotional study* enables the Christian to understand the word of God and practise it.

As Christians, then, we cannot escape from the necessity of Bible study. To encounter God in his word involves more than a lazy, passive approach to the Bible. If this book is to be the talking book God intends it to be, we must examine the jewel of the Scriptures with regular study.

Under such scrutiny, the text takes on a significance hitherto unknown. The word of life burrows down and buries itself into the heart. A verse or word suddenly sparkles with light. Like a precious stone, it is carefully lifted out of its context and examined. Attracted by its beauty, we engage in the art of meditation. The subtle interplay of light in the gem of Scripture becomes the light of God's revelation to the individual; the word of the Lord becomes a word for us today.

We conclude this chapter where we began. The Holy Spirit, using all our various gifts of logic, perception and imagination, speaks to us as we confront the word that he originally inspired. To hear God speaking is not passive, but demanding and difficult. Encountering God in his word, we hear the voice that called our universe into existence. Powerful, penetrating, ancient yet resonant with life and creation, his word is never silent. He calls to us from his talking book.

Notes

[1] Thomas à Kempis, *The Imitation of Christ* (Penguin: Harmondsworth, 1952), p 92.
[2] Madame Guyon, *Experiencing the Depths of Jesus Christ* (Christian Books: Augusta, Maine, 1980), p 8.

3 Cheslyn Jones, Geoffrey Wainwright, Edward Yarnold (eds), *The Study of Spirituality* (SPCK: London, 1986), p 567.

4 *Hagah* is used to describe a lion growling over his prey (Is 31:4); the moaning of a dove (Is 38:14); a synonym for 'to speak' (Ps 37:30); to indicate reflection (Ps 143:5).

5 Jean Leclercq, *A Dictionary of Christian Spirituality* (SCM Press: London, 1983), p 261.

6 Jim Packer, *Knowing God* (Hodder and Stoughton: London, 1973), p 20.

7 Leclercq, *op cit*, p 262.

8 Francis de Sales, *Introduction to the Devout Life* (Image Books: New York, 1950), p 83.

9 Tony Buzan, *Use Your Head* (Ariel Books: London, 1974), p 60.

7

The Language of Intimacy

'Orare est laborare—to pray is to work.'
Benedictine motto

Prayer has been described by the saintly Andrew Murray as the 'pulse of life; by it the doctor can tell the condition of the heart'.[1] Prayerlessness indicates, then, that there is something seriously amiss in our Christian experience. In reconciling us to himself through the death of Christ, God has given us the gift of prayer. Enemies have become friends; God and man can communicate together.

In all its diverse expressions, prayer is the language of intimacy with God. It begins with the glad cry of recognition, *'Abba*, Father', and develops into the mature relationship of an adult son or daughter with the divine Parent. To engage in prayer is the most sublime and exalted of all human activities. The intercessor transcends his earthly limitations and is welcomed into the family life of the Godhead. Each of the divine Persons is dynamically and personally involved, aiding, inspiring and answering our prayers (Rom 8:26–27; Jn 14:13; Rom 8:34; 8:15–16).

The intimate Father/child relationship provides the theological and experiential basis of prayer. Human beings, responding to the call of Christ, have become the adopted children of God. This intimacy between Father and child must never degenerate into disrespectful familiarity. The introduction to the Lord's

Prayer, 'Our Father in heaven, hallowed be your name', holds an important clue to our approach to God. As 'our Father', he desires an intimacy and warmth of relationship, but as 'our Father in heaven', he demands our obedience and respect. God exudes the same sense of danger that one associates with an electric power station. The coils, the cables and the huge generators indicate enormous power. To trespass or handle without the proper caution can be fatal. Similarly, to approach God without the proper reverence indicates an ignorance of his majesty and power. The approach to God involves both the invitation, 'Come!', and the warning, 'Beware!' He is both our Father and Judge, our Friend and Master, our Bridegroom and Creator.

Prayer is only occasionally a cosy fireside chat with God. 'God is a consuming fire,' writes Ruth Burrows, 'and my filth crackles as he seizes hold of me; he is all light, and my darkness shrivels under his blaze. It is this naked blaze of God that makes prayer so terrible.'[2] As we approach God, all the elaborate defence mechanisms that conceal the real person are disengaged. Alone and vulnerable, like a tortoise without its shell, we encounter our Creator. Our finite lives are plunged into the infinite glory of the Godhead. In the act of prayer, we align ourselves with the Sovereign Will that governs this universe. No longer the impotent children of time, we become part of the unfolding drama of God's reign on earth.

By birth, we belong to the natural order of star, planet, animal, reptile and molecule, but this is not our true vocation. Beyond the visible, material creation is the transcendent universe of the Triune God and his holy angels. Prayer gives us access to this other kingdom. Immersed in the glory of God, we share in the government of the planet. In prayer, we regain our crowns. Taking our stumbling words and inarticulate longings, God turns them into the edicts of his purposes. To pray is to join ourselves to God in his reign over the universe.

Prayer and the supernatural

Writing to the Roman church, Paul says,

> In the same way, the Spirit helps us in our weakness. We do not know what we ought to pray, but the Spirit himself intercedes for us with groans that words cannot express. And he who searches our hearts knows the mind of the Spirit, because the Spirit intercedes for the saints in accordance with God's will (Rom 8:26–27).

The word translated 'help' in verse 26 is only used on one other occasion in the New Testament. It means to take part with, to come to someone's aid. The Holy Spirit encourages prayer, co-operating with us in this ministry. Moreover, when we are incapable of finding the language to express our deepest longings, the Holy Spirit prays on our behalf. The groans of the Spirit, unintelligible to the Christian, are understood by God.

The recognition of the limitations of the intellect is a well known phenomenon. In prayer, we encounter the ineffable. Our finite minds are numbed by the sheer wisdom and greatness of God. Thomas Merton uses the analogy of a rocket to express this feeling of inadequacy:

> Mental prayer is therefore something like a skyrocket. Kindled by a spark of divine love, the soul streaks heavenwards in an act of intelligence as clear and direct as the rocket's trail of fire. Grace has released all the deepest energies of our spirit and assists us to climb to new and unsuspected heights. Nevertheless, our own faculties

soon reach their limit. The intelligence can climb no
higher into the sky.[3]

It is at this point in our experience that the rocket
explodes in a dazzling display of coloured stars and
thunderclaps. 'The intelligence can climb no higher';
the Holy Spirit intervenes. Our knowledge of God's
will may be imperfect, our language stumbling and
confused, our prayer lacking in clarity and perception,
but aided by the Spirit, weak words become powerful
and potent. Like a poorly worded essay a tutor
rewrites, the Holy Spirit rewrites our prayers in a
language acceptable to heaven. Those scattered and
incoherent words and phrases that arise from our
hearts reach the ears of the Father as compositions of
beauty and lucidity. The Holy Spirit translates our
desires to the Father in a clear and intelligible manner.
Evaporation largely purifies water; even water from a
muddy pool will become as clean and pure as a mountain spring after evaporation has taken place. The
Spirit takes our weak and faltering prayers, purifies
them, and presents them to the Father transformed.

The emphasis on praying in the Spirit has important implications (Eph 6:18; Jude 20). Prayer is a supernatural exercise, and our conversation with God can
be directly inspired by the Holy Spirit. A significant
element in true prayer is the capacity to share in the
feelings of God. To view prayer as a form of calm
detachment is to misunderstand this ministry. Prayer
often results in a violent fluctuation of emotion: joy in
God, pain in the suffering of the world, sorrow over
sin, and times of intense darkness and conflict. In his
journal, David Brainerd frequently uses words such as
'agonise', 'wrestle' and 'burden' to describe his
experience of prayer. His experience is by no means
unique, and all who take prayer seriously will sometimes be called to share in the agony of God for his

church and world. As in any satisfying relationship, friendship with God involves participation in his feelings. Through prayer, God shares himself with his children. To intercede is to discover both the power and vulnerability of God.

The Holy Spirit lifts us to a totally new level of prayer. Thought and organisation are important, but these are no substitute for sensitivity to the Spirit's guidance. God can give the most remarkable insights as we pray for individuals, the church, world mission and matters of international importance. In fellowship with the Holy Spirit, our humble prayers can become prophetic. This supernatural element in prayer can make the ministry unpredictable. The Holy Spirit can awaken the Christian in the middle of the night, or unexpectedly seize him with a deep desire for prayer. This kind of prayer is far removed from the 'wishbone' variety that attempts to control God by an endless tirade of petitions. To pray in the Holy Spirit is not to control God, but to be controlled by him. God, not ourselves, becomes the focus of prayer.

Difficulties in prayer

Prayer is the most widely encouraged ministry, but sadly, the most neglected. There is no simple answer to this anomaly. To attempt to analyse every cause of prayerlessness is quite beyond me, but it's worth mentioning some of the most common.

Satanic opposition

To kneel in prayer is to attract the antagonism of the devil. Here, more than in any other ministry, we influence the invisible conflict that rages in our world. Certainly Christ has won the victory on the cross and now reigns omnipotent, but this is no justification for complacency. A philosophy of history that disregards this spiritual dimension, explaining events in purely natural terms, is misguided. Insane forces seek to drag the human race to extinction. History is a Jekyl and Hyde, a frightening collusion of the diabolical and the sane.

For the Christian, the cross signifies the decisive overthrow of evil. Through the death of Christ, God 'disarmed the powers and authorities' that rule the planet (Col 2:15). Prayer is both the acknowledgement of this victory and its enforcement. No wonder the praying Christian invites the relentless attack of hell. The sudden explosions that rip through the mind, the compulsions that demand instant satisfaction, the darkness and depression, and the succession of interruptions all indicate demonic harassment. To kneel does not signify merely surrender to God, but defiance to any power that attempts to usurp his rule. Prayer is thus both the affirmation of our loyalty to God, and a declaration of war against Satan and all his works. Unprepared for such determined resistance to our prayers, we quit the battlefield.

Materialism

The continuing economic success of Western Europe depends partly on rampant consumerism. The underlying premise is that the quality of one's life depends on the accumulation of possessions. Much in the West is commendable. I, for one, am grateful for a comfortable house, central heating, a reliable car and all the other benefits of 'civilisation'. The danger, however, is that the Christian can be so comfortable that the kingdom of God loses its attraction. The life of the Spirit is slowly throttled by an idolatrous love of material things.

During my childhood, my mum would often sing me to sleep with a lullaby. In spite of all my determined attempts to remain awake, the gentle and melancholy notes of the song would weaken my resolve. Sleep crept upon me so quietly that I could never identify the moment when it pounced and bore me away. My eyes, heavy with sleep, held Mum's face until the effort became impossible to sustain. Like a closing door, my eyes shut. The lullaby had summoned me to sleep's mysterious kingdom. Only on waking to the grey light of dawn did I know that I had been asleep. Eight hours had passed in a moment. My only memories were the tiny fragments of dreams, washed up like flotsam on the slender shoreline of my mind.

An inordinate love for the material things of this world can be exactly like a lullaby—sending us into a state of spiritual stupor and eventually to sleep. For the Christian, the temptation to compromise with mammon, to coexist with the world, to invest in the consumer paradise of Western materialism, has never been stronger.

The Christian is a spiritual refugee. He loves this planet and may fight for justice and truth, but he does not ultimately belong here. The Scriptures refer to us as 'aliens and strangers in the world' (1 Pet 2:11), indicating that our 'citizenship is in heaven' (Phil 3:20). Our predicament is simple: we serve God and humanity in this world, but long 'for a better country—a heavenly one' (Heb 11:15). Heaven is the homeland of our hearts. But materialism can dull our spiritual homesickness. Prayer, however, is the language of a church besotted with God. If our loyalties are divided between the world and the kingdom, prayer will become more difficult. The lullaby of the world is much harder to resist than my mother's song. It sounds seductively in our hearts, calling us to forsake our first love for God and squander our affections on material things. If we succumb to the song, we will be lulled to sleep. Prayer will lose its delight and power.

Instant results

In little more than a century, the pace of life has accelerated dramatically. Sadly, God has become a victim of the technological revolution. Prayer is seen as a kind of celestial drinks machine. Provided the correct coins are inserted and the appropriate button pushed, God is obliged to respond immediately. Hey presto, an answered prayer shoots into our waiting hands.

Certainly, God responds to some prayers immediately. When Peter was sinking in the Lake of Galilee, Jesus didn't wait around before answering his prayer. Peter's desperate cry, 'Save me!', elicited an instant response. Any delay by the Lord might have drowned his leading disciple. George Muller, the founder of the Bristol children's homes, claimed that he had received 30,000 answers to prayer either in 'the same hour or same day that the prayer request was made'.[4] So God sometimes does answer prayer promptly; but other prayers are answered only after years of determined effort.

The paradox of prayer is the tension between faith and persistency. To be effective, prayer requires faith. Jesus says, '...whatever you ask for in prayer, believe that you have received it, and it will be yours' (Mk 11:24). (I will explore some of the meanings of faith on pp 127–130.) Faith, however, is not the only condition of answered prayer. Jesus advocates tenacity and persistence (Mt 7:7–8). This importunity of prayer is illustrated in two of his most well known parables: the friend at midnight (Lk 11:5–10), and the account of the widow and the unjust judge (Lk 18:1–8).

Prayer is not an instant, painless occupation. A 'push button' approach to prayer will result in disillusionment. If God does not answer our petitions immediately, we can lose interest in prayer. Persistence builds character and patience into the Christian. Faith that persists through years of discouragement and darkness is faith indeed.

True prayer clings to the promise of God until it is rewarded with the answer.

The pain of self-knowledge

My daughter has invented (or rediscovered) a game. She stands conspicuously in the centre of the room covering her face with her hands. 'Daddy! Daddy!' she cries, 'I'm hiding!' As long as her face is covered, she assumes she is invisible. Her logic is very simple: if I can't see Daddy, he can't see me.

Our attitude towards God can be reminiscent of my daughter's approach. Provided we cover our faces and pretend he cannot see us, we are able to maintain the illusion that our sin and self-deception are hidden from him; but prayer removes our hands from our faces and forces us to look at God. In his brilliant light, there are no hiding places. We can no longer find refuge in self-deception and self-justification. The truth of God stings like antiseptic in an open wound. If we can bear the pain and bitterness of self-discovery, the truth of God will bring healing and renewal. If not, we will always fear prayer and avoid it.

Prayer has been described as the true self meeting the true God. If our true self is covered with the graveclothes of pride and unresolved sin, prayer will always bring bitterness and pain. I am convinced that this is one of the main causes of prayerlessness. To pray is to be found out, to be stripped of all deceit and unreality, and to stand naked and vulnerable before God.

Some practical suggestions

Prayer is much more than a series of petitions. It includes worship, confession, silence, petition, intercession, liturgical prayer, warfare with Satan, and the more inarticulate expressions such as tongues. The Scriptures recommend that special times should be set aside for private prayer (Mt 6:6), but this should not lead to a schizoid attitude in which the Christian only prays in private, neglecting to pray at any other time. 'Pray continually' is Paul's instruction to the Thessalonians (1 Thess 5:17). Commenting on this truth, Vladimir Lossky writes: 'Prayer must become perpetual, as uninterrupted as breathing or the beating of the heart.'[5]

There is in fact no tension between private prayer and the continuous prayer encouraged in the Bible. Indeed, the first provides the impetus for the second. The vital difference between human and the divine relationships is that God is always with us. When friends engage in a conversation, the exchange of information can only continue during their time together. Every question, intimacy and item of interest must be squeezed into the available time. This pressure does not exist with God. Writes A.W. Tozer:

> Eternal years lie in his heart. For him, time does not pass, it remains, and those who are in Christ share with him all the riches of limitless time and endless years. God never hurries. There are no deadlines against which he must work. Only to know this is to quiet our spirit and relax our nerves. For those out of Christ, time is a devouring beast; before the sons of the new creation, time crouches, and purrs and licks our hands.[6]

The truth that we 'live, move and have our being' in God removes the hysteria from Christian living. The constraints of time that regulate human relationships and activities do not exist with God. As people of time, we are governed by the schedules and deadlines of our society. But we are not prisoners of the system. We inhabit the kingdom in which none of these restrictions applies. Once we choose to follow Christ, eternity has seized us. God is with us all the time. Our prayers can be spread throughout the day or night because he has promised never to leave or forsake us (Heb 13:5).

How then do we establish a life of private prayer?

Cultivate a sense of God's presence

Chapters 4 and 5 have already explored the theme of practising the presence of God, but we do not always *feel* God's presence, and at such times to pray into an apparent vacuum can be disconcerting. Undoubtedly, there will be times when God will seem close; but on other occasions he will seem distant and remote. At such times, we must hold him firmly in our hearts by faith, refusing to allow our feelings to dictate the terms. Julian of Norwich, writing as if God is speaking, offers us this encouragement: 'For when you are dry, empty, sick or weak, at such times is your prayer most pleasing to me.'[7]

Writing requests

Gordon Jeff gives wise advice when he writes, 'To sit down with a pen and paper rather than simply to think and pray, can be an aid to concentration and productivity.'[8] The tendency for the mind to wander during times of prayer can be averted by writing not only a journal (as described in Chapter 6), but also our requests. Moreover, writing enables the intercessor to think more clearly about his petitions, avoiding the temptation for prayer to become self-preoccupied— one's own needs taking precedence over the worship of God and the needs of others.

Some writers distinguish between *petition* and *intercession*. The former signifies prayer for one's own needs (Phil 4:4–7), whereas the latter refers to prayer made on the behalf of others (1 Tim 2:1–2). I am not convinced that such definitions are altogether scriptural, but they can be useful. True prayer has the cross at the heart of it. 'The Christian life,' writes Catherine of Genoa, 'is nothing else but a continuous cross and a continuous prayer.... Without the cross, all our prayers avail nothing, save to cause us to live lives of even deeper self-deception.'[9] Writing can be a form of self-surveillance, identifying the time spent in prayer for self and others. The cross should painfully end our self-orientation, freeing us to reach out to others. Many requests are vague and unspecific. 'God bless Mary!' may be a fine sentiment, but what does the speaker mean? Writing helps our prayers to become more specific and intelligent. The rather inane 'God bless Mary' is replaced by a more carefully considered request. Mary's needs are analysed from every conceivable angle and translated into fervent prayer.

Resources for prayer

Like any other activity of life, prayer requires careful organisation. Prayer letters, photographs, newspaper and magazine articles, the news, and books like Patrick Johnstone's excellent *Operation World* can provide material for prayer. Prayer is not an escape from the world, but an invasion of the world, so the Christian with a sensitive social conscience can bring international events to God in prayer. He can stand with the children of famine in Ethiopia, attend the East-West summit on nuclear disarmament in Geneva, live among the poor in the slums of Mexico City, and fight for racial justice in South Africa.

Faith

Without faith prayer is futile. John Watson, the eloquent Puritan preacher, writes, 'Prayer is the key of heaven; faith is the hand that turns it.'[10] If prayer is not joined with a living trust in God, our prayers will be useless.

Faith is not something that we work up, the religious equivalent of the bravado of a man who stands on the window-ledge of his twelfth-story apartment repeating, 'I can fly!', and who, when he has generated sufficient faith in his aeronautical abilities, leaps into space. Faith is not self-hypnosis or a positive mental attitude, but an attitude of humble, adoring trust. Faith derives its power from its object. 'Have faith in God' enjoins the Lord Jesus (Mk 11:20–25). It is not great faith that is important, although this is commended in Scripture, but faith in a great God. Without the reality of a personal God, faith would be little more than wish-fulfilment.

Faith must never be viewed as the carte blanche that obliges God to fulfil our every wish. A faith that strays from the word of God is presumptuous. There are two important elements in the faith/word relationship. Faith should be rooted in the general promises of Scripture. For example, in praying for one's daily needs, we have the promise that God will care for all our practical necessities (Mt 6:25–34). There are other occasions when the way is not so clearly illuminated. Guidance for the future is a case in point. In such a circumstance, God can either give a direct word to indicate his will for us, or leave us in darkness and uncertainty. In the latter case, prayer becomes more difficult. Commonsense, natural aptitudes and personal preference may suggest a certain line of action, but it is not always clear whether this is the will of God or not. Prayer becomes an enquiry rather than a deliberate request. The answer, when it comes, may take the form of circumstances. Faith is still present in this type of prayer; we are trusting God to pilot us to safe moorings although the navigation lights do not appear to be shining.

Pauline and I discovered this clearly when, during a cycle marathon from Lands End to John O'Groat's, we encountered terrible weather. Only fifty miles from our destination, the conditions deteriorated badly. We were hurled across the road by savage gusts of wind. The rain was torrential, driving into and stinging our faces with such ferocity that we felt as if we were being attacked by a mad acupuncturist.

Pauline became angry with God. 'If you're the Creator,' she prayed, 'why don't you do something about this miserable weather?'

There was no immediate response to Pauline's prayer. We endured the day with a grim determination, seldom speaking or smiling, our faces as bleak as the storm that beat against us. The answer to Pauline's prayer came three years later, on another journey and in another place.

Disgorged from the express after a five-day journey, courtesy of Indian Rail, our first priority was food: not the inedible snacks and endless cups of sweet tea that had sustained us during the long hours of the journey, but real food: tandoori chicken, lamb masala, *rogan josht*, and any other delicacy that a top class restaurant could offer.

'Disgorged' is probably the best word to describe the sudden decisive jolt that heralded our arrival at Howrah station, Calcutta, and the irresistible confluence of people and luggage that bore us from the train into the bedlam of this old city.

Darkness had fallen and the stars hung in constellations from the night like glittering chandeliers. The city burned with light. The twinkle of neon signs, the searchlight beams of passing cars, the flickering of bicycle headlamps, and the warm, inviting light that flooded from bus windows all gave Calcutta an exotic, feverish magnificence. The night cleansed the city of its poverty and squalor; tragedy was hidden by darkness.

Boarding a bus that would take us to the finest restaurant in the city, we happened to look out of the window to the street below. It took our minds seconds to process what we saw. Unable to accept it at first, we experienced a rush of emotion: unbelief, amazement, outrage, and finally that cold moment of truth when one realises that what one sees is, in fact, undeniable reality. I wept, biting my lip in embarrassment, hiding my face so that the other passengers would not witness my grief.

Beside the stiff and putrid corpse of a dog lay a man. Starvation and illness had wasted his body. His skin, stretched tightly over his skull and ribcage like cling film, had a transparent quality. Death will take us all, but this was an obscene way to die. A few metres from the gutter which served as his bed, people stood or crouched to urinate. In all the millions of that city, no one seemed to care. It was this indifference, this utter disregard for human suffering, that made his condition so terrible.

As I tried to make sense of what I was seeing, God spoke to my wife. It had taken him three years and 5,000 miles to answer her prayer. 'What was your suffering,' he said, 'compared with this?' She remembered the wind-driven rain of the Scottish Highlands and recalled her own discomfort and resentment against God. In comparison to the agony of this man, her sufferings were trivial. The pain and hardship of Calcutta was God's answer to her prayer. He spoke through circumstances.

Even as you keep a record of your prayers, expect answers. To list our petitions and tick off answers can

be a simple, yet effective way of increasing our faith
and enthusiasm for God. One of the most joyful
experiences of the Christian life is a positive answer to
prayer. Those who are reluctant to take prayer seriously will be strangers to this very special sign of the
Father's favour.

Asceticism and prayer

The church has often maintained an uncomfortable
relationship with the body and its desires. Influenced
by Greek dualism, spirituality and the desires of the
body have often been considered as opposed to one
another. Manacled to the desires of the body, the soul
can only attain freedom by a rigid process of asceticism and self-discipline. Bonaventure, a typical example of someone with this approach, refers to this
ascent of the soul as 'the six steps of the true
Solomon's throne, by which we arrive at peace'.[11]

Gluttony, fornication and all indulgence in fleshly
lusts are rejected in Scripture, but such prohibition
does not imply that the physical desires are wrong and
therefore harmful to the life of prayer. Like a car
which, if it is to perform reliably, requires strict
adherence to the manufacturer's recommendations,
the bodily appetites only find true fulfilment in obedience to God. Hedonism, far from bringing freedom,
leads into an arid waste of guilt and frustration.

Even today, the church is fidgety about the
appetites of the body. Such nervousness reflects an
often dark and miserable history. Origen, the Church
Father, castrated himself in a fit of religious fervour;
Augustine forbad sex for pleasure within marriage;
Saint Benedict's solution to the lusts of the flesh was to
cast himself naked into a thorn bush! 'There,' wrote
his biographer, 'he wallowed so long, that when he
rose up all his flesh was pitifully torn: and so by the

wounds of his body, he cured the wounds of his soul.'[12] Peter Levi, in his book *The Frontiers of Paradise*, refers to the fashion for 'insanitary spirituality', citing Theodore of Sikyon as an example. This devout hermit spent two years in a cave. When he eventually came out, 'his body was skin and bone, covered in sores and worms, his hair matted and horrifying, and no one could come near him because he stank so badly'.[13]

One of the most extreme ascetic movements of the Middle Ages was the wrongly named 'Friends of God'. In the interest of piety, the followers of this movement subjected themselves to the most brutal self-torture. With their constitutions weakened by flagellation and fasting, they became highly susceptible to psychic manifestations. The lesson they learned is common to all such movements: starve and beat the body, and the mind becomes hallucinogenic. Of course, such extremism is rejected in Scripture. The body with all its appetites is described as 'very good' (Gen 1:31), the temple of the Holy Spirit (1 Cor 6:19). Discipline of it is recommended, but this is not a licence for self-abuse (1 Cor 9:24–27). In fact, Paul, writing to the Ephesians, dismisses the suggestion altogether: 'No one ever hated his own body, but he feeds and cares for it, just as Christ does the church' (Eph 5:29).

The appetites of the body are not the enemies of Christ. To deny their existence or attempt to repress them can do incalculable damage to the life of the spirit. To reject one's sexuality, or, for that matter, any other bodily appetite, is to quarrel with the Creator. In creating us 'male' and 'female', God made sexuality integral to our identity. Gender is his idea.

You may be asking, 'What does all this have to do with the subject of prayer?' The desires of the body, legitimate in themselves, can intrude into our relationship with God. Self-denial is not popular in the

West. The playboy philosophy of self-indulgence is generally accepted, supported by media hype and trendy psychology. Moreover, among many Christians there is a loss of personal discipline. To counter this tendency, the Scriptures advance two forms of self-denial: temporary sexual abstinence (1 Cor 7:5) and fasting (Mt 6:16–18). Neither discipline is compulsory, but their inclusion in Scripture suggests that their practice is important. The reason for such self-denial is twofold: to give more time to prayer, and to subordinate one's desire for food and sex to the will of God.

There is always a danger that the insistent and compulsive demands of the stomach and the craving for sexual satisfaction can take precedence over the life of prayer. The apostle Paul compares himself to an athlete who, in his determination to win the race, subjects his body to regular training (1 Cor 9:27). A disciplined body is an excellent servant, but if its appetites become renegade, it can be a tyrannical master. Fasting and sexual abstinence are two ways by which the desires of the body can be controlled, freeing us to concentrate all our energies on prayer. This does not imply that sexual intercourse and a healthy appetite are inimical to a vocation of prayer. Indeed, to refuse sexual intercourse to one's spouse is not a sign of superior spirituality, but of disobedience and possible neurosis (1 Cor 7:1–7).

The enjoyment of God certainly does not imply the abandonment of all human pleasures, for the Scriptures teach that God 'richly provides us with everything for our enjoyment' (1 Tim 6:17). The temporary suspension of sexual activity within marriage and the relinquishing of food do not indicate that either activity is wrong. Both, however, must be subordinate to the desire for God. The rapture of lovers and the enjoyment of food must never be despised. A spirituality that is unable to accommodate the physical and sensuous elements of human experience is dangerous and unscriptural. Prayer is not an escape from the physical world, but a recognition of its importance. The Incarnation is God's rebuttal of such a view, his affirmation of the goodness and beauty of the created world. The Lord who reigns over the universe is both divine and human. He has taken upon himself our humanity, and lifted it to the highest place of all.

Of the two disciplines, sexual abstinence and fasting, the latter is by far the most common. In Scripture, reasons for fasting include humbling oneself before God (Ps 69:10), repentance (Joel 1:14; 2:12), a thirst for God that makes eating unimportant (Ps 42:3), prayer (Acts 13:2–3), and self-denial (Ps 35:13).

Fasting is not usually injurious to health providing three factors are taken into consideration: first, health—the person who fasts must be healthy; second, rest—the person who fasts must not be engaged in any strenuous activity; and third, time—the risks increase the longer the person spends in fasting. Of course, fasting is inadvisable for anyone in poor physical or mental health, or employed in some form of manual labour. Diabetics, hypoglycemics and those suffering with stomach ulcers are particularly vulnerable and must consult their doctor before starting a fast. All strenuous physical activity should be suspended for the duration of the fast. With reserves of blood sugar depleted by fasting, we become susceptible to the cold and do not have our normal strength and endurance. With these exceptions, a fast of up to five days would be unlikely to damage the health; but if you intend to fast for more than five days, do seek responsible medical advice.[14]

The initial period of a fast is often accompanied by delicious smells from the kitchen, usually quite imaginary. Denied its regular intake of meals and snacks, the stomach and saliva glands are driven into a frenzy. The fast, practised to encourage prayer, may have the reverse effect. So intense are the hunger pangs that one becomes too distracted to pray with passion and concentration. Like Esau, we are willing to sell our inheritance for a plate of stew (Heb 12:16). Fortunately, this period is usually of short duration. The longer one fasts, the weaker becomes the stomach's protest. The benefits are enormous: power in prayer, clarity of vision, intimacy with God, freedom in worship, and a sense of moral elation—the body has been disciplined in the service of the spirit.

If this description sounds too much like a TV commercial, I will interject some advice. Fasting is not a magic formula. In order to derive the maximum benefit from it, preparation, careful thought and determination are required. If, for example, you are in the habit of spending only ten minutes with God alone each day, it is hardly advisable to spend an entire day in prayer and fasting. To do so would be rather like attempting to swim the English Channel when you have only recently managed to swim a width of the swimming pool. Begin by giving up one meal and use the time in prayer. With more experience, the period spent in fasting can be extended.

Prayer is the spark that sets us aflame for God.

Notes

1 Andrew Murray, *The Prayer Life* (Lakeland: Basingstoke: 1981), pp 14, 19.
2 Ruth Burrows, *Ascent of Love* (Darton, Longman and Todd: London, 1987), pp 63–64.
3 Thomas Merton, *Spiritual Direction and Meditation* (Anthony Clarke Books: Wheathampstead, 1975), p 45.

4 Roger Steer, *George Muller: Delighted in God* (Hodder and Stoughton: London, 1965), p 301.

5 Vladimir Lossky, *The Mystical Theology of the Eastern Church* (James Clarke: London, 1957), p 204.

6 A.W. Tozer, *Knowledge of the Holy* (James Clarke: London, 1965), p 52.

7 Julian of Norwich, *Revelations of Divine Love* (Penguin: Harmondsworth), p 124.

8 Gordon Jeff, *Spiritual Direction for Every Christian* (SPCK: London, 1987), p 50.

9 Cited in Bede Frost, *Mental Prayer* (SPCK: London, 1954), p 176.

10 John Watson, *The Lord's Prayer* (Banner of Truth: London, 1972), p 275.

11 Bonaventure, *The Soul's Journey into God* (SPCK: London), p 110.

12 Cited in Betrand Russell, *A History of Western Philosophy* (Alan and Unwin: London, 1979), p 375.

13 Peter Levi, *The Frontiers of Paradise* (Collins Harvill: London, 1987), p 45.

14 For further information on fasting consult David R. Smith, *Fasting: A Neglected Discipline*; Arthur Wallis, *God's Chosen Fast* and Richard Foster, *Celebration of Discipline*.

8

The Business of Heaven

'Joy is the serious business of heaven.'

C.S. Lewis

The instrument

From the dust of the earth, God created an instrument of worship supreme in the natural world. Only the angels excelled in splendour. Made from the same molecules as the birds, fish, animals and other living creatures, it was different in one important respect: it had been made in the likeness of God; the image of the Creator had been blazoned upon it. This creation united heaven and earth.

The instrument was like none other ever created. It could reason, think, make deliberate choices and itself create things of beauty. Tuned by the Creator, its music was so tender and lovely, so resonant with praise and simple majesty that angels danced at the sound of it, and the Trinity cried out in joy.... But all that was untold centuries ago.

Obsessed with its own uniqueness and the twisted ambition to become God, the instrument made music for itself and forgot the One who formed it. The song it plays today is of a different kind. Some of the ancient genius and originality survive, but its music is full of grief, despair and wickedness. The song has filled the earth with war and misery; the joy of heaven has become a bitter funeral march of death and sorrow.

The 'instrument' here, of course, represents man (I will use the generic title for men *and* women), and his destiny to worship God. 'The primary purpose of God in creation,' writes A.W. Tozer, 'was to prepare moral beings spiritually and intellectually capable of worshipping him.' [1]

In creating man, God brought into existence a being with the capacity to love him of his own free will. Without this freedom, love would have been meaningless, and the kind of worship God envisaged impossible. If we define love as the appreciative and sacrificial response of one person to another, the possibility of rejection will also exist. Love, by definition, allows freedom, and the fact that man was specifically created to love God does not nullify this argument. From the moment Adam's eyes opened to the face of his Creator, he loved him with the natural, spontaneous love that a child gives a caring parent. In loving God, he was merely fulfilling the purpose of his existence. Ignorant of sin and the demonic darkness that would soon sweep the human family, he loved God with a sincerity and simplicity unspoilt by self-will and pride. His was the innocent enjoyment of an unfallen creature loving God because it was his nature to do so.

Self-love: inverted worship

The catastrophic event described in popular theology as the Fall changed the orientation of love. Before the disobedience of Adam and Eve, their lavish talents of intellect, emotion, imagination and creativity found supreme expression in the adoration of God; but their rejection of God superimposed a dark and grim negative over the creation idyll. Man's capacity for love and worship was redirected; man proudly usurped the Creator's throne. Deceived by Satan's lie, '…you will be like God' (Gen 3:5), he squandered his love upon himself. In essence, self-love is merely inverted worship.

Rather than elevating man morally and spiritually, this self-love is degenerative. The prodigy of creation becomes a dangerous renegade. In its more bizarre and psychotic manifestation, self-love gave birth to the Nazi super race ideology of Hitler and his Third Reich; and in its more acceptable disguise to the rampant self-centredness of the consumer society.

Rejecting his Creator, man has deified himself. Even his gods are little more than a projection of his own personality. The heaven of fallen men and women becomes populated with larger-than-life animations of themselves. Heaven becomes a Hollywood of celestial superstars. The need for worship, this persistent tug heavenwards, makes man incurably religious. His destiny as an instrument created to worship calls out to him. He cannot deny the call without invalidating his existence, so he forges gods in his own image and bows down to worship them.

The commandment that we should love God with all our heart, soul, mind and strength (Mk 12:29–31) is given to restore our love to its proper object: God himself. Self-love has twisted and deformed the image of God within us to such an extent that we have become a parody of our Maker. This ugly, crippled thing that has filled the earth with war and torment was once God's perfect instrument.

But Christ's advent was intended to salvage men and women and begin a new creation in the midst of the old. By giving his blood as a ransom for our sins, the Lord Jesus purchased us from slavery and made us his very own possession (1 Cor 6:19–20). The call of Christ is not merely one of forgiveness but of self-denial. Jesus insists that 'whoever wants to save his life will lose it, but whoever loses his life for me will find it' (Mt 16:25). A love squandered on self is a prodigal, misspent love.

Without submitting to the daily discipline of the cross, there can be no true worship. Western life (as we have noted already) militates against a life of self-denial. I suspect that self-denial has become unfashionable because we see God as a 'super commodity' reigning in a consumer heaven. For very little investment on our part, he will provide happiness, success in business, lovely feelings of warmth and acceptance; heal our headaches and heartaches and send us sweetly to sleep at night. Much of Western Christianity has become effete and lazy.

How easily we can be brainwashed by the propaganda of our age and opt for a God who demands nothing and yet gives everything! This God of popular mythology has been divested of his majesty and sovereignty and now fits comfortably into the world of TV commercials and advertising campaigns. He has been spruced up, given an acceptable public image, has been taught the slick and sly language of the professional communicator. He is only too happy (we imagine) to give his blessing in exchange for a ballot box 'X' next to his name; ironically, this 'cross' is the only one he requires of his followers! In this modern caricature of biblical Christianity, God bears a closer resemblance to the politician canvassing for votes at a general election than the awesome, uncompromising Deity who springs from the pages of Scripture and from the beauty of his creation.

We would do well to hear the warning of John Preston: 'If you love the Lord for your own good, it is a false love, but if you love him for himself, simply without any respect for the recompense of reward, then it is love indeed.'[2] Johann Arndt is even more daring in his analysis of the problem: 'Man was made to love nothing but God alone. And since that God is to be loved alone, it follows that he who loves himself is an idolater, and makes himself God.'[3] The obsession with self that is so much a part of Western Christianity is a dangerous and insidious form of idolatry. Grown fat on our blessings and the rich legacy of our history, we need to feel again the torment of the nails and the pain of the cross.

A God of utility?

The seductive view of God as political candidate or manager of a convenience store is highly dangerous to the Christian life. According to the Scriptures, the universe exists for the pleasure of the Creator (Rev 4:11). The enjoyment of God must therefore never be confused with self-interested covetousness. Instead, to love God requires the abandonment of self-love (Mt 16:25). As Creator, he demands our obedience for no other reason than that we belong to him.

Thankfulness and appreciation of God for his gifts are both authentic elements of worship, and as such should not be despised. To enjoy God for his gifts alone, however, is unsatisfactory. God desires to be loved for himself (Ps 27:4; Phil 3:8). Our highest enjoyment should not be the pursuit of personal happiness, but the longing to give pleasure and joy to God. The aphorism 'It is more blessed to give than receive' applies as much to our relationship with God as it does to our relationships with others.

Apotheia—passion in worship

The disregard of one's own needs to give pleasure to God was referred to by the Desert Fathers as *apotheia*. Originally the meaning conveyed by the word was that of the suspension of human passion, but in the theology of the Desert Fathers it was used to express the idea of inner purity. *Apotheia* refers to that condition of heart in which all fleshly lusts and longings have been transcended by passion for God. This is what Jesus meant when he said, 'Blessed are the poor in spirit, for theirs is the kingdom of heaven' (Mt 5:3). The person who has painfully relinquished the addictive cravings of the flesh will inherit God's kingdom (1 Jn 2:15–17). Paradoxically, to surrender to being poor in spirit results in an inheritance of the incalculable riches of God. To lose ourselves so that we can find God and give him pleasure is the crowning act of our humanity, the reason for our existence.

Even the contemporary stress on worship can be self- rather than God-centred. In the act of worship, self-gratification and fulfilment can be more important to the Christian than glorifying God. The success of worship may be determined by the worshipper's feelings—did he have nice sensations?—and not by the pleasure our heavenly Father derives.

The existential and consumer-oriented nature of Western society has made the subjective elements of Christianity attractive. Experience has become more important than objective truth, and this obsession with experience has influenced the outlook of the church. Even the modern revitalising of worship owes as much to this cult of subjectivism as it does to the work of the Holy Spirit.

Delight and joy in God's presence are undoubtedly a central part of worship, but we must never confuse these with thrills, titillations and exciting feelings. Thomas à Kempis instead exhorts us to true worship:

A loud cry in the ears of God is that burning love of a soul which exclaims, 'My God and my love, you are all mine, and I yours.... Let my soul spend itself in your praise, rejoicing for love. Let me love you more than myself, and myself for your sake.'[4]

This desire to love God more than self runs like a seam of gold through all the classics of devotional literature. Clearly, true worship demands the renunciation of self-love if the Christian is to engage in the selfless worship of God. Love for God and a twisted love for self cannot coexist in the same soul. Self-love, cleverly disguised with the stage makeup of pseudo-piety and religiosity, can pass as the worship of God. The language of praise can be polished and eloquent, the emotions refined, the voice suitably hushed and reverent or raised in whoops of joy—but there is little of the rapt adoration and delighted wonder that characterise the true worshipper.

Self-love can tiptoe into this most sublime of human activities. Communion with God then becomes little more than religious self-indulgence, and worship a soliloquy of selfishness. In my own prayer-life, I have to struggle constantly against this tendency. My own needs, problems, and ambitions can take precedence over the desire to adore God. The only antidote to this addiction to self is constant vigilance and the application of the cross: the daily dying to self, surrender to the will of God, and the deliberate, conscious decision to put God's happiness and wishes before my own.

The meaning of worship

The main group of words in the Hebrew and the Greek of the Bible translated as 'worship' denote reverence, submission and service; and by implication, the adoration of God. John Baigent writes that worship in 'its widest sense must denote the whole of the life of the individual viewed as service to God, orientated towards God, submitted in obedience to his will, with everything being done to glorify him' (1 Cor 10:31; Col 3:17).[5]

Although this chapter will concentrate on the private and verbal aspects of worship, I would like to emphasise that worship is far more than words in secret. According to the apostle Paul, the 'spiritual worship' of the Christian is 'to offer your bodies as living sacrifices, holy and pleasing to God' (Rom 12:1–3). True private worship is only viable if the whole of one's life is offered to God as a living sacrifice. Wrote Ramon Lull:

> To thee alone I offer and present myself, that I may serve thee. Whatever may become of me, let it be to this end, to wit thy praise, honour and glory. Thee alone do I fear, from thee alone is my strength, for thee I weep, for thee I burn with love, and none other Lord will I have save thee only.[6]

These words of Lull's are a striking illustration of Paul's meaning. The most eloquent worship does not spring from the lips, but from a life utterly yielded to God and his word.

Joy

The Bible is ecstatic with the praise and adoration of God. While recognising the benefit of silence as a tool for listening and contemplation, we must realise that God desires the verbal praise of his people. On occasions, worship can rob us of the power of speech as we gaze enthralled at the majesty of God, but the normal response is one of joyful, abandoned praise. The Franciscan, Jacopone da Todi, describes this ecstasy of joy in a poem entitled 'On the Heart's Jubilation', and demonstrates that it must find expression in worship and singing:

> Joy shooting upwards uncontrollably,
> Where is the heart to contain it?

O shouting and singing oblivious to all,
Joy brimmed to overflowing![7]

The Scriptures encourage singing (Ps 95:1), shouting (Ps 95:1), dancing (Ps 149:3), clapping (Ps 47:1),
hand raising (Ps 63:4), kneeling and prostration (Ps
95:6) in the practice of worship. The introduction in
recent years of some of the more physical styles of
worship such as dancing and clapping is hardly new.
Autobiographical sections of many of the great writings of the church describe the joy of God being
expressed in a tangible, physical manner. In 1904 in
the Welsh revival, God's people spontaneously
danced as they were filled with the Spirit of God. To
be touched by the fire of God's love can precipitate
unusual responses. Only a church frozen into respectability by the extreme cold of God-deprivation will
react negatively to extravagant and adoring worship.
God is not tame and respectable—not the infinite
projection of all those qualities of quietness, reserve
and emotional repression that supposedly characterise
the British personality. No, he is a dangerous, irre-
sistibly beautiful Being. One glance of his eye can
penetrate the veneer of respectability and traumatise
our hearts into breathless, delirious song. Even as I
write, I want to cry out with joy. How can one be silent
and restrained before such majesty?

Christian emotional repression can find expression
in other outlets. A friend of mine, a Baptist with a
deep suspicion of any emotional display in worship,
invited me to attend a football match with him. At first
I said no. I thought the enthusiasm and unrestrained
emotionalism of the crowd would send him into a
prolonged state of shock, but my fears proved ground-
less. As we mixed with the crowd, he underwent a
dramatic change of personality. This usually phlegma-
tic and taciturn man was transformed into a singing,

combative and eccentric football supporter. The joy on his face and the gleam of expectation in his eyes were so different from the plastic, expressionless mask he wore on Sundays.

The next two hours were a complete revelation. Taking a position at the very front of the stand, my friend maintained a non-stop commentary on the progress of the game. The commentary included uncomplimentary and derisory descriptions of players and their skills, rebukes to the referee, and gusts of such passion that he would have been immediately signed up by a Brazilian TV network if one had been present at the match.

For my friend, football was a catharsis. Here, with thousands of chanting 'worshippers', he could sing, shout, and cheer—yet preserve his anonymity. All the repressed emotions of fear, aggression, resentment, anger, joy and triumph were permitted. Without football, he would have been a time bomb, ready to detonate at a touch.

I am not recommending worship as a catharsis for the emotionally repressed. My point is simple and I hope obvious. The healthy and natural expression of emotion is allowed in almost every activity except that of worshipping God; here it is considered to be fanaticism. Fortunately there will be no such restraint when we gather round the throne of the Lamb in the New Jerusalem.

Joy in church history

One of the most striking characteristics of the great saints of history is their delirious joy in God. Francis of Assisi is referred to as 'heaven drunk'; Symeon, the Eastern Father, describes being 'overwhelmed with tears and inexpressible joy and exultation';[8] John Ruysbroeck, the medieval theologian and man of God, writes:

A man receives more sensible joy and sweetness than his heart can either contain or desire. It makes some sing and praise God because of their fulness of joy, and some weep with great tears because of their sweetness of heart. It makes one restless in all his limbs so that he must run, jump and dance; and so excites another that he must gesticulate and clap his hands. Another cries out with a loud voice and so shows forth the plentitude he feels within; another must be silent and melt away, because of the rapture he feels in his senses.[9]

Whitefield, the burning evangelist of the eighteenth century, is described by an observer as being in an 'ecstasy of joy',[10] and David Brainerd, the missionary to North American Indians, writes in his diary:

My soul rejoiced with joy unspeakable to see such a God, such a glorious divine being, and I was inwardly pleased and satisfied that he should be God over all, forever and ever. My soul was so captivated and delighted by such loveliness, greatness and other perfections of God that I was swallowed up in him.[11]

The experience of joy in God is not restricted to a privileged elite, an exclusive club of 'supersaints' within the church, but is the legacy of all true children of God. Reading an account of the Welsh revival of 1904, I came across a brief but telling description of a man's encounter with God. So overwhelming was his joy that he could write, 'I have found myself laughing for hours on end...I feel I can pray by laughing these days.'[12]

Joy in Scripture

Such joy and delight in God need not be uncommon among us. The Scriptures swarm with references to enjoying God. This is not something marginal or rare, but crucial to Christian experience. Some of the most sublime and ecstatic language in the Bible is inspired by the joy of encounter with God. After one of the most bleak and depressing prayers of the Bible, Habakkuk suddenly bursts into jubilant song. 'Yet I will rejoice in the Lord,' he cries, 'I will be joyful in God my Saviour' (Hab 3:18). The Hebrew language of the Old Testament is replete with words that express joy and rejoicing. Ecstatic joy, however, is not restricted to the Old Testament. Peter, writing to the Jews of the Diaspora, says, 'Without having seen him you love him; though you do not now see him you believe in him and rejoice with unutterable and exalted joy' (1 Pet 1:8, RSV). Peter uses two interesting Greek words in this verse. The first, *agalliao*, translated 'rejoice', is a rare word in the New Testament. Walter Bauer's lexicon gives the meaning as 'to exult, to be glad, to be overjoyed'. *Agalliao* therefore describes an ecstatic state of mind and spirit (Lk 1:47; 10:21; 1 Pet 4:13; Rev 19:7). The second word is the Greek *chara*, translated 'joy'. The word signifies gladness and is the most common delineation of joy in the New Testament. Both words are brought together by Peter in an attempt to express the 'inexpressible and glorious joy' which is the legacy of the child of God.

The popular myth that every true Christian should behave as if he had a severe attack of headache has no precedent in the New Testament. The encouragement to rejoice in God is a consistent motif throughout the Bible (Rom 14:17; Gal 5:22; Phil 4:4). God is jubilant, vibrant with life and eternally joyful. To enjoy God is to share the deep resonant joy of the divine Being. If we are to enjoy God as he desires, we must learn to think biblically. The serious, austere God of respectable evangelicalism bears little resemblance to the majestic, living Lord of the Scriptures.

Worship and the Godhead

Worship begins with a vision of God. The person who
has encountered God can do little else but worship
him. When the women saw Jesus on the resurrection
morning, they clung to his feet and worshipped (Mt
28:8–10). The worship of our Triune God should not
merely be the response to his gifts, but to God himself.
This desire for God unites all traditions of spirituality.
'Oh show me yourself that I might love you' cried the
Puritan John Preston. His words have been the prayer
of all the lovers of God throughout time.

To understand God exhaustively as we understand
(say) a machine is, of course, impossible. The
attributes of God revealed in the Scriptures are all that
we can begin to grasp in our fallen, finite condition. In
encounter with God, joyful recognition is combined
with a sense of mystery and awe. This sense of mystery and incomprehensibility has been described by
theologians as the 'ineffability of God'. In fact, in the
Eastern tradition of spirituality, the mystery of God
has given rise to an approach called the 'negative way'
(Latin, *via negativa*). In this approach, God is
described negatively as the 'mysterious darkness',[13]
the 'hidden silence',[14] the 'abyss'[15] and even a 'desert'.[16] When we are united with God, it is argued, we
encounter a Being so unlike ourselves that human
language and illustration are totally inadequate to
define him. Worship is reduced to a perpetual state of
silence before eternal mystery.

Admittedly, silence is an element of true worship,
for in every authentic encounter with God, delight in
his self-revelation is combined with that elusive sense
of mystery and awe. The danger occurs, however,
when silent contemplation is elevated above verbal
praise.

To define silence as the most elevated form of worship is to fly in the face of overwhelming scriptural

evidence. From the earliest chapters of the Bible, the reader is confronted by a jubilant company of people who express their delight in God by singing, shouting, clapping, dancing and playing an assortment of musical instruments. Their God is not a mystical abstraction perpetually surrounded by darkness and shadow, but the Triune Creator whose self-revelation fills the universe with praise and glory. Yes, silence is a component of worship, but the predominant theme of Scripture is of joyful, uninhibited praise and adoration. The God who delights in his creation and describes it as 'very good' has given us bodies with which to serve him, and tongues to extol the honour of his name: 'I will extol the Lord at all times; his praise will always be on my lips' (Ps 34:1).

The experience of God

Encounter with God is central to biblical revelation. As we open the pages of the Bible, we are permitted to witness the most holy and elevated of spiritual experiences. We see Moses encountering God in the simplicity of the burning bush, and later, in the thunder, fire and cloud of Sinai (Ex 3:1–6; 19:18–19); we share Ezekiel's vision of the chariot throne of God (Ezek 1), and cry out with Isaiah 'Woe to me' as we gaze upon the holy splendour of the 'King, the Lord Almighty' (Is 6:1–6). Falling on our faces with John, we shield our eyes from the terrible majesty of the Son of Man (Rev 1:12–18); and with the apostle Paul, we stumble blindly to the dust, smitten by the lightning and glory of the risen and exalted Jesus (Acts 9:1–9). The Bible is the book of God, the self-revelation of the Triune Majesty who desires fellowship with men and women.

Encounter with God puts the passion and the wonder back into worship. The individual who encounters

God is confronted by a Being of such infinite power
and glory that the senses ignite and blaze with divine
fire. This 'holy madness' must never be confused with
insanity or a condition of psychological disturbance. It
is the healthy and natural response of the human
spirit to the revelation of God. Knowing our weakness
and incapacity, God loves us gently. If he were to
show us the full splendour of his face, we would
explode in a conflagration of love and jubilation. As it
is, he gives himself to us according to our capacity to
receive: a loving glance, a kind smile, a song of joy in
the night, a swift embrace, a ray of light filtering
through the crack in the door between heaven and
earth. But even that 'little light' is sufficient to ignite
our senses with the fire of love.

If this description seems overly poetic and unreal, it
might be useful to recall one's reaction to the more
dramatic experiences of life: watching a sunset in the
mountains, listening to a thunderstorm on a summer's
night, admiring the beauty of the countryside in late
spring, falling in love, one's marriage and the birth of
a child. These experiences do not leave one unmoved
and indifferent. Their uniqueness and wonder elicit a
spontaneous response of laughter, tears, breathless
admiration or wild, ecstatic joy. If our reaction to the
natural things of the world can be dramatic, how
much more the response to the Creator's self-dis-
closure. Before such blinding light, the most beautiful
aspects of creation appear as grey shadows, things of
no consequence. The beauty of this world is surpassed
by that of the next. Human love with all its tenderness
and sexual delight becomes a mere shadow of the
divine love and its eternal consummation in heaven. It
is as if we hold a tiny match which flickers in the
darkness. Knowing nothing else, we remain content
with its weak illumination. But when we see the sun,

the light of our match is darkness by comparison. We discard it for the better light.

The wound of love

The spiritual writings of the church, irrespective of denomination bias and theological eccentricities, are vibrant with this burning love for God. Without it, worship is dull and formal, the words of a song bereft of music and feeling. The soul that has been touched with the fire of God's presence will be ablaze with love for him. Until such a time, we are dry tinder, potentially combustible but in desperate need of the Spirit's consuming fire.

The Spanish saint, John of the Cross, wrote poetically of the love of God:

> O living flame of love
> that tenderly wounds my soul
> in its deepest centre.[17]

'This flame of love,' he continues, 'is the Spirit of the bridegroom, the Holy Spirit.'[18] This concept of the 'wound of love' is certainly not unique to John. As early as the third century, Origen could write of the 'dart and wound of love' in his commentary on the Song of Songs.[19] Jacopone da Todi, already quoted in this chapter, refers to it as 'O happy wound, full of delight'.[20] When the Holy Spirit truly fills the Christian, he inflicts a wound of longing on the heart. This 'wound of love' is the natural outcome of encounter with God. The fire of the Spirit cauterises the lust for the world and fills the heart with a deep longing for God.

A church crippled by materialism can only be healed by the rediscovery of God's presence. Without that, the consumer 'durables' and values of Western civilisation will infringe on the life of the Spirit. The greatest threat to the Western church is not liberalism, secularism, or even the occult, but rampant and unbridled materialism. Bereft of the experience of God, we fix our hearts on mammon and the toys and gadgets of the manufacturing industry.

It is impossible to overestimate the importance of the Spirit in worship. 'He alone,' writes Tozer, 'can raise our cold hearts to rapture and restore again the art of true worship.'[21] According to the Scriptures, the Spirit inspires worship (Jn 4:24), allows access to God (Eph 2:18), enkindles us with the fire of love (Rom 5:5), fills us with the joy of the kingdom of heaven (Rom 14:17) and satisfies our hearts with the vibrancy of the divine presence (Jn 4:13–15). Paul's instruction, 'Do not get drunk on wine, which leads to debauchery. Instead be filled with the Spirit' (Eph 5:18), is not something peripheral to the Christian life, but indispensable. I have never yet read a great Christian autobiography or devotional classic without being impressed by the centrality of the Holy Spirit. Arndt refers to his fullness as 'holy drunkenness',[22] Bernard of Clairvaux as 'that drunkenness which is sobriety',[23] and D.L. Moody, the nineteenth-century evangelist, as a baptism of love so intense that he asked God 'to stay his hand'.[24] If we are to worship God as he desires, then, it must be 'in Spirit and truth'.

Problems and helps

Some readers may be discouraged by my insistence on encounter with God. The depth and variety of encounter described in this chapter may be light years from your experience. Rather than motivated and inspired, the chapter has left you stunned and discouraged. The kind of relationship envisaged here is perhaps as remote and elusive for you as the mythical pot of gold at the end of a rainbow. How then do we find it?

Encounter with God is not attained by discipline and asceticism but is the gift of God's grace, a God who desires intimacy with his children. So intense and overwhelming is this love that God offered up his Son in sacrifice in order to win our hearts. Our wrong perceptions of God and sense of guilt and unworthiness can rob us of the pleasure of his company. Like a child who is doubtful of her father's love, we can be afraid to approach him, fearing his rejection and indifference. Regrettably, this attitude can rob us of a lifetime of intimacy with God.

A human analogy of a man obsessively in love with a woman serves to illustrate. The woman comes from a wealthy family and is his social 'superior'. This cultural difference, however, makes no difference to the woman's feelings towards the man. She loves him with all her heart and wants to marry him. But so awed is he by the woman's beauty and superiority that he is unable to believe that she really loves him. His sense of inferiority precludes him from a happy and satisfying relationship with her. What should have been a joyful and intimate union of lovers becomes extremely painful for them both.

Our experience of God can follow a similar pattern. Our reluctance to believe God has forgiven and accepted us can deprive us of the very intimacy he yearns to bestow. Worship, as the most tender expression of this intimacy, becomes a formal and embarrassing exercise. True worship, on the other hand, is rooted in the certainty that God loves us and will never stop loving us.

Worship involves the abandonment of self-will and submission to God. The motive of worship, therefore, is not our personal happiness, but the glory and pleasure of God. Authentic spiritual experience has nothing in common with the modern cult of sensation. Drugs, eroticism, fast cars and other stimulants may be used to 'satisfy' this craving; cocaine or an unusual erotic encounter may give the monotony of one's life a fleeting 'meaning'. Man is the ultimate consumer. Experiences are either purchased or obtained illegally to enhance the grubby squalor of his life. Living in the centre of an artificial, selfish universe, he relates to life in terms of what he can *get out of it*. His religion, if he has one, is the religion of self-fulfilment and self-realisation. The world and all in it exists for one purpose: to satisfy him and give him happiness.

Such an attitude is the antithesis of the worship of God. To relegate God to the level of a life-enhancing experience is to miss the whole point of Christianity altogether. Granted, to encounter God is crucially important for the Christian, but to worship the experience rather than God himself is to do irreparable damage to the life of the spirit. Seek God and his pleasure even if this sometimes means darkness and aridity, and your worship will bring delight to him.

Do not allow feelings alone to dictate your worship and praise. The Scriptures encourage us to 'continually offer to God a sacrifice of praise' (Heb 13:15). All of us have times when we feel numb and indifferent towards God, but these occasions must never deter us from worship. The onus is on the will. Praise is not something that we do when we feel good. The purpose of worship is to give God pleasure and joy. His feelings should come before our own.

Attempt to make praise and thanksgiving a habitual part of your life. Worship is not restricted to special times and places but is the attitude of the heart to God. A Christian who is helplessly in love with God will express adoration at every opportunity. Try to change the ordinary and mundane activities of human existence into continual praise and worship. Surrender all activities to God as an act of worship, recognising that the most humble action, if performed for his glory, gives him pleasure. Above all, seek to be filled with the Holy Spirit. It is his ministry to fill our hearts with the love of God and inspire our tongues to praise. The language of the Spirit-filled man is the language of worship.

Give time during your private devotions to worship. A.W. Tozer would regularly spend an entire day in worship. Charles De Foucauld wrote in his journal, 'More than fifteen hours with nothing to do but to gaze on you, Lord, and tell you that I love you.'[25] With family responsibilities and the incessant demands of modern life, the luxury of such a time with God is remote. However, the principle is important. Love for God requires time to appreciate him.

Prayer, worship and confession—the subject of Chapters 6, 7 and 8—are so closely related that to sever one results in an imbalance. The interior life of the Christian cannot be regulated by rules. It is impossible to say what proportion of time should be given to each component. On one day, worship may be the main feature of our prayer; on another, God deals with us and we spend a prolonged period in confession of sin; on yet another occasion, a need for prayer may drive us to our knees in intercession. Circumstances can also determine the content of our prayer. A particular trial, a family problem, an emergency or a tragedy can make us cry out to God for help. In my own prayer-life, I usually begin with confession, then engage in worship, and conclude with petition. This pattern, however, is regularly disrupted. The method, then, need not concern us too much.

Worship, confession, and intercession are the means by which we respond to God and co-operate with him. Of the three, worship will continue into eternity.

Notes

1 A.W. Tozer, *Born After Midnight* (Christian Publications: Harrisburg, Pennsylvania, 1959), p 10.
2 John Preston, *Sermons* (1638), p 26.
3 Johann Arndt, *True Christianity* (Joseph Downing: 1720), p 99.
4 Thomas à Kempis, *The Imitation of Christ* (Penguin: Harmondsworth, 1952), pp 98–99.
5 John Baigent, *Declare His Glory* (Paternoster Press: Exeter, 1988), p 14.
6 Raymon Lull, *The Art of Contemplation* (SPCK: London, 1925), pp 48–49.
7 Jacopone da Todi, *The Lauds* in *The Classics of Western Spirituality* (SPCK: London, 1982), pp 227–228.
8 Cheslyn Jones, Geoffrey Wainwright, Edward Yarnold (eds), *The Study of Spirituality* (SPCK: London, 1986), pp 239–240.
9 John Ruysbroeck, *The Adornments of the Spiritual Marriage* (J.M. Dent: London), p 69.
10 Arnold Dallimore, *George Whitefield*, (Banner of Truth: London, 1980), p 128.
11 Shirwood Eliot Wirt (ed), *Spiritual Awakening* (Lion: Tring, 1986), p 121.
12 Eifion Evans, *The Welsh Revival of 1904* (Evangelical Press: London, 1969), p 111.
13 Dionysius, *The Complete Works* in *The Classics of Western Spirituality* (SPCK: London, 1987), p 137.
14 *Ibid*, p 135.
15 John Tauler, cited in Michael Cox, *Mysticism* (Acquarian Press: Wellingborough, 1983), p 109.
16 *Ibid*, p 109.
17 John of the Cross, *Selected Writings* in *The Classics of Western Spirituality* (SPCK: London, 1987), p 293.
18 *Ibid*, p 295.
19 Origen, *An Exhortation to Martyrdom, Prayer* and *Selected Writings* in *The Classics of Western Spirituality* (Paulist Press: New York, 1979).

20 Da Todi, *op cit*, p 236.
21 A.W. Tozer, *That Incredible Christian* (Christian Publications: Harrisburg, Pennsylvania, 1964), p 131.
22 Johann Arndt, *True Christianity* in *The Classics of Western Spirituality* (SPCK: London, 1979), p 259.
23 Bernard of Clairvaux, *On the Love of God* (Mowbrays: London, 1961), p 50.
24 John Pollock, *Moody Without Sankey* (Hodder and Stoughton: London, 1966), p 87.
25 Cheslyn Jones, Geoffrey Wainwright, Edward Yarnold (eds), *The Study of Spirituality* (SPCK: London, 1986), p 421.

9

Treason and Pardon

'It is not the constant thought of their sins, but
the vision of the holiness of God that makes the
saints aware of their own sinfulness.'

Anthony Bloom

The aweful presence of God brought a wave of conviction
of sin that caused even mature Christians to feel their
sinfulness.... Strong men were bowed under the weight
of sin and cries of mercy were mingled with shouts of joy
from others who had passed into life.[1]

The event thus described took place in the Isle of
Lewis in 1949. The revelation of the 'aweful presence
of God' resulted in the recognition of sinfulness and
sincere confession and repentance.

At the heart of the gospel is the doctrine of forgiveness. In that most famous of all parables, about the
prodigal son, God is depicted as a father whose son
has gone into a far country, but now returns in disgrace, his fortune wasted. What will the father do? He
forgets his dignity in the joy of his son's return, runs
to meet him, hugs and kisses him and then prepares a
banquet in his honour. God reveals himself as the
forgiving Father.

The purpose of this chapter is to show that this
forgiveness only becomes available when we confess
our sins to God. It is not sufficient to repent of our sins
at conversion, neglecting to confess those sins that we

subsequently commit. The Scriptures teach that we must keep a short account with God, constantly confessing our sins and joyfully receiving his forgiveness. Confession, therefore, is the means by which we 'spring-clean' our lives in order to make them habitable by God.

Confession must never be confused with a morbid kind of introspection. It is the heart's response to the holiness of God. As bright sunlight exposes grime on a window, the glory of God reveals our sins to us. Confession is the means by which we clean the window of the soul in order to admire the beauty of God. Without regular confession of sin, our lives will quickly revert to their former darkness.

Only as we recapture a vision of God's majesty will sin assume the repulsive characteristics that the Scriptures attribute to it. Knowledge of sin springs directly from personal encounter with God. To gaze into his face is to tremble with both love and fear. It is this subtle blend of emotion that elevates relationship with God above all others. The greatness and moral perfection of his character provoke reverence and holy fear, while his love and mercy welcome us into fellowship and union with himself.

The Scriptures are clear that sin separates from God and provokes his anger. While benefiting from forgiveness and the gift of the Spirit, the Christian is still vulnerable to temptation and sin. To maintain an uninterrupted relationship with God, therefore, requires regular confession.

The First Epistle of John shows us that the blood of Christ sustains us in the presence of the Father: '...the blood of Jesus, his Son, purifies us from every sin' (1 Jn 1:7). The Christian life, therefore, is one of continuous confession and continuous reconciliation. Without the cross, confession would be meaningless.

The cave of the tiger

The 'gentle Jesus meek and mild' of Sunday school days bears little resemblance to the just and holy God of the Bible. In the Old Testament alone there are twenty different words that describe the wrath of God and over 580 references to his judgement. This insistence on the holy anger of God against sin is carried over into the New Testament (Jn 3:36; Rom 1:18; Eph 5:6; Rev 11:18; 14:10; 16:19; 2 Thess 1:7–9). The word 'wrath' does not denote a capricious God who loses his temper every time we sin, but a consistent and vigorous attitude of antagonism towards evil. Wrath, therefore, can best be described as the holy rage of love, God's unequivocal moral outrage against sin and disobedience.

Sin is not only a threat to God's creation, but an attack against his very nature and integrity. Such a violation of his character and law inevitably provokes his anger. Even in its most 'innocent' guise, sin is an act of treachery against the Sovereign Majesty of the universe.

To be true to God, we must try to grasp his love and wrath. Both attributes are integral to the character of God. If we overemphasise the retributive elements of God's nature, ie, wrath, justice and judgement, we portray him as a revengeful tyrant, the spiritual counterpart of a Hitler or Nero. Conversely, if we exaggerate the love and mercy of God, denying his purity and holiness, we portray our heavenly Father as a sentimental, morally neutral and innocuous Deity, hardly worthy of our respect and worship. Morton Kelsey was correct when he wrote:

We have to turn away from the idea of popular sentimentality about God being loving. Freud was certainly right in criticising that kind of religion, which he described as a longing to return to the womb. It expresses a desire to be taken care of by an indulgent parent without conscious consideration of what life is about.[2]

To relegate the Creator Lord of the universe to the level of a poodle or harmless lap-dog is to be guilty of sacrilege. God was not boasting when he said to Moses, 'No one can look at me and live.' For all his love and grace, God exists in 'unapproachable light' (1 Tim 6:16).

The consuming fire

The God of the Bible is also described as a 'consuming fire' (Heb 12:29). He is not a safe and predictable Deity, but one who blazes with holiness. The caricature of God as a slightly dotty, eccentric old man in a flannelette nightgown must be firmly rejected. This senile heavenly father has as much in common with the living God as a doormouse to a leopard or a lion. The God of the Bible is terrible and dangerous (Ps 119:119).

The idea of holiness includes the uniqueness of God, his separation from creation, and the moral splendour of his attributes. By reason of his eternity and infinity, he transcends all our categories of space and time. Perfect and unendurably beautiful, he radiates such a complete and intense purity that the whole of the created order appears unclean by comparison. So dangerous and terrible is this holiness that God hides himself from us. If we were to be confronted with his naked majesty and splendour, like a tiny insect flying into a forest fire, we would be instantly incinerated. To see God as he is in his holiness is to die.

Wrath and love are not, however, diametrical opposites. In fact, so closely are love and holiness related that the love of God can be rightly described as a 'holy love'. Even the biblical idea of the wrath of God is not inimical to love. The wife who returns home and finds the husband that she loves with another woman will be legitimately angry. During her journey home she may have passed a number of other couples without the slightest feeling of apprehension or anger, but love for her husband turns his infidelity into something considerably more serious. The sheer intensity of her love and desire for him makes his disloyalty the ultimate act of betrayal. Rage at his deception and infidelity is merely an expression of her love. Indifference to his adultery would indicate the absence of any deep feeling or concern for him. Similarly, the 'wrath of God' is an expression of his love. Sin, even the most trivial, provokes the rage of God and suspends relationship with him. Only by confession can the relationship be restored.

My first experience of God's holiness was disturbing. Sitting in my father's study reading the prologue to John's Gospel, I was suddenly overwhelmed by the divine presence. It was as if a blinding flash of light had cut through the darkness of my mind and senses. Two emotions fought for mastery within me. The first was the desire to escape from the burning light; the second was fascination. That special sense of holiness stripped me of all self-deception and pseudo-spirituality. I saw both my insignificance and the sordid nature of my life.

The strange and elusive interplay of emotion that accompanied the encounter is difficult to put into words. I felt much like a chronically sick patient who is suddenly confronted by a person full of health and vitality. In the presence of such wholeness, I felt crooked and crippled, withered and blighted. Repulsion and fascination struggled together in my soul. Fortunately, fascination won the day; that I might to some degree share in his holiness has become the desire of my heart.

The appropriate response to the holiness of God is reverential fear. The fear of God, however, must never be confused with the hysteria of a victim before a murder weapon strikes him down, or the cold panic that paralyses mind and body in the moment before a serious accident. The fear of God is an entirely different experience. This 'religious feeling of terror,' writes Walter Eichdrodt, 'does not have the character of panic nor even of servile anxiety, but contains a mysterious power of attraction which is converted into wonder, obedience, self-surrender and enthusiasm.'[3]

If we are to make confession a serious part of our devotional life, we must cultivate an awareness of God's holiness. The quality of fear that springs from this encounter is a great deterrent to sin. Any 'experience of God' that does not deepen our self-knowledge and shatter our self-deception could well be spurious.

Loss of the sense of divine majesty

The loss in some churches of the sense of the divine majesty—and concomitantly, the loss of the doctrines of sin and confession—can be attributed to several factors. Not least among them is the subtle and pervasive influence of Western culture and thought upon the theology and outlook of the church. Psychotherapy in some cases has tended to undermine the concept of moral responsibility. The blame for anti-social and evil behaviour has shifted from the individual to past experiences, to the environment and other external or unconscious influences. While recognising the contribution of modern psychology to an understanding of human behaviour, we must never lose sight of the biblical view of man as a sinner. The notions of rebellion and moral guilt do not fit comfortably into secular Western thinking. There is a very real temptation to accommodate the gospel to the popular outlook. Jesus becomes 'my shrink' rather than 'my Saviour'.

Obsession with sin has been described as the dangerous neurosis of Christianity. Some secular thinkers have caricatured us as a people preoccupied with guilt. Our sin fixation is considered by some to be a pathological disorder. Without the Christian doctrine of forgiveness, this accusation would be justified; and in response to the charge it is important to remember two things: first, recognition of sinfulness springs from encounter with a holy God; second, awareness of moral guilt is no more serious than the recognition of a physical disorder.

Guilt provoked by a sense of God's majesty can be compared to the body's nervous system. If we place one hand in a fire, the burn inflicted results in instant withdrawal. If for some reason, however, the sense of pain is suspended, the body can be ignorant of its danger. Pain is the body's early warning system. Guilt fulfils a similar function in the conscience. Each time we sin, the conscience responds with guilt. The purpose of guilt is curative rather than condemnatory. It is not an unhealthy personality disturbance, but the recognition of our moral imperfection. It drives us to our knees before Christ to ask for forgiveness.

A second reason why we have lost the sense of God's majesty and holiness is the rarity of wonder and awe. Toffler speaks of the shock of a people catapulted into the future with such alarming speed that they are incapable of coping with the kaleidoscope of change. Confronted by a never-ending side-show of technological marvels and scientific discoveries, we freeze in numbness and shock. The capacity for surprise and astonishment is slowly lost. The 'numinous' to which Otto refers in his book *The Idea of the Holy*,[4] has become the 'normal' today. The majestic, mysterious God of the Bible is merely another marvel ranking with the microchip, Haley's Comet, lunar exploration, satellite TV and nuclear power.

Our capacity for wonder and incredulity has stretched to such a degree that we are incapable of little more than a tired grunt of appreciation when confronted by the idea of the glory of God. Like spoilt children, we have so many toys to play with that we quickly become bored and our attention span limited. In the consumer wonderland which is Western society, we have become a bored, listless and empty people. Apathy has become the most universal emotion. Unfortunately, perception of God has fallen victim to the same attitude. Malachi's description of the religious malaise of his day could well apply to our society: 'A son honours his father, and a servant his master. If I am a father, where is the honour due to me? If I am a master, where is the respect due to me? says the Lord Almighty' (Mal 1:6).

The awareness of God's majesty and holiness cannot be conjured up like the genie in Aladdin's lamp. He desires to reveal himself to his children, but will come near only to the humble and broken-hearted who are sincere in their longing for him. Through study of the Bible, meditation, prayer and silent contemplation, we must attempt to recapture the holy dread of God, the awesome sense of the divine majesty and the realisation of our 'infinite distance' from him—as well as our intimacy with him.

The practice of confession

Honesty

Richard Rolle, a shrewd judge of character, advises the Christian 'not to pretend to a holiness that is not yours'.[5] The idea that the Christian should be a spiritual superhero who never sins has resulted in an unhealthy form of triumphalism. Richard Foster makes a very significant point when he writes:

> Confession is so difficult a discipline for us partly because we view the believing community as a fellowship of saints before we see it as a fellowship of sinners. We come to feel that everyone else has advanced so far in holiness that we are isolated and alone in our sin.... Therefore we hide ourselves from one another and live in veiled lies and hypocrisy.[6]

The unwillingness to be honest about our sins, however, must not be attributed to this factor alone. T.S. Eliot draws attention to the human aptitude for self-deception. In his poem, 'Burnt Norton', he writes, 'Human kind cannot bear very much reality.'[7] To live happily with ourselves seems then to require self-deception; the recognition of sin can be too painful for our self-esteem. To protect a fragile ego and identity, we resort to self-righteousness, justifying sin by an appeal to circumstances or by delegating blame to others. This tendency is as old as the human race itself. Adam excused his sin by saying that Eve was responsible for his disobedience (Gen 3:12).

John, writing in his First Epistle, exposes this tendency to deceit and dishonesty:

> If we claim to have fellowship with him yet walk in the darkness, we lie and do not live by the truth (1 Jn 1:6).

> If we claim to be without sin, we deceive ourselves and the truth is not in us (v 8).

> If we claim we have not sinned, we make him out to be a liar and his word has no place in our lives (v 10).

The logic in John's argument is that to refuse to admit

our sin is to be dishonest and self-deceived. Moreover, by insisting on our own righteousness, we disagree with God's verdict, indirectly accusing him of lying.

Owning up to sin can be traumatic, shattering years of self-deception and escapism. But only when the pseudo-self is destroyed can the new person, 'created to be like God in true righteousness and holiness' emerge (Eph 4:24). Beyond the pain and anguish of self-realisation is the joy of discovering a new identity in God.

Because men and women are social beings, a basic human need is acceptance. This need for acceptance often results in dishonesty. We are afraid to expose our moral temptations, struggles and failures to one another in case of rejection. The depth of relationship that we yearn for can, as a consequence, elude us. So strong is the desire for approval, acceptance and self-acceptance that we cover our true self with the skilful application of the cosmetics of lies and deceit. The face that we present to others can be little more than a painted clown's mask replete with an artificial smile.

There can be no cover-up with God. The irrational urge to paint over our sins is futile. His love will not tolerate such deceit. Confession begins when we come out of hiding and stand alone and vulnerable before God. To attempt to hide our sins from him is probably the most dangerous kind of self-deception. He knows all things. 'You have set our iniquities before you, our secret sins in the light of your presence' (Ps 90:8). God is too realistic to expect us to be perfect, but he desires sincerity and honesty.

Contrition

The purpose of conviction of sin is not to drive us into the despair of self-loathing and hatred, but to lead us to confession and repentance. The Greek verb translated 'repent' *(metanoeo)* signifies a drastic change of mind and direction, rather than a mere apology for wrongdoing.

I was brought up in a tradition where women were encouraged to remain silent in church and wear some form of head-covering. Almost in defiance of this regulation, the women turned hat-wearing into an elaborate art form. Weird and wonderful creations of gauze, swirling, starched linen, a peacock array of coloured ribbons, and the inevitable bunches of faded fabric flowers all adorned their heads. Sunday worship could have been in danger of becoming a fashion show.

To stop these masterpieces from flying off in anything but a totally draughtless atmosphere, women kept them in place by wicked-looking hat pins. Once, on returning from church, my mother made the mistake of leaving one of her selection of hat pins on the mantelpiece. The mistake was further compounded by my father, who was bending down when I noticed it. Never a boy to fight temptation, I stole over to the mantelpiece and removed the pin. Tiptoeing to my dad, I drove the pin into his bottom. The leaps, yells, cries, groans and wild hand-raising anticipated the liberty of the charismatic movement by at least ten years.

After discipline had been administered to the same part of my anatomy that had given my dad so much discomfort a few minutes earlier, I was told to pray for forgiveness. 'Dear God,' I said in a subdued whisper, 'forgive me for driving that pin into Dad's bottom.' I paused for effect, long enough for Dad to interject a loud 'amen'. 'Please Lord,' I continued, 'never let me get caught again!'

Confession is not a convenience that enables us to escape the moral consequences of deeds so that we can

commit the same sins again. John Woolman, the eighteenth-century Quaker who fought for the abolition of
slavery, wrote in his journal, 'I sought deserts and
lonely places and there, with tears, did confess my
sins to God, and humbly crave help of him.'[8] Woolman's qualifying clause, 'with tears', indicates that his
confession was not shallow and insincere. He experienced remorse over his sins. In Psalm 32, David
describes the pain that preceded his confession:

> When I kept silent
> my bones wasted away
> through my groaning all day long.
> For day and night your hand was heavy upon me;
> My strength was sapped as in the heat of summer
> (Ps 32:3–5).

Under conviction of sin, his conscience could only be
relieved by confession and the assurance of forgiveness:

> Then I acknowledged my sin to you
> and did not cover up my iniquity.
> I said, 'I will confess my transgressions to the Lord'—and
> you forgave the guilt of my sin (v 5).

Without contrition, confession is almost meaningless. 'Godly sorrow,' writes Paul, 'brings repentance'
(2 Cor 7:10). The purpose of contrition is to give us a
proper understanding of the gravity and seriousness
of sin. Confession is the language of a broken heart (Ps
51:17).

The words of Hosea, 'break up your unploughed
ground' (Hos 10:12), have often been applied to the
barrenness of the human heart. The writer to the
Hebrews warns of the danger of unconfessed sin.
Mutual encouragement to holiness is recommended if

the heart is not to become 'hardened by sin's deceit-fulness' (Heb 3:13).

For the Christian, persistence in sin can result in the malfunction of the conscience. What was once alive and sensitive to the rebuke of the Holy Spirit can become dead. If we do not take advantage of regular confession, the spiritual life can become as fruitless and barren as an unploughed field. Soil that should yield the fruit of the Spirit becomes overgrown with weeds and thorns. The only solution to such an infer-tility of life is the plough. 'The church that fears the plough,' writes A.W. Tozer, 'writes its own epitaph; the church that uses the plough walks in the way of revival.'[9] In the language of the metaphor, the action of the plough represents contrition and confession of sins. Only by the regular use of the plough can the soil of the heart be sufficiently broken up to yield fruit.

Confession and cleansing

The Greek word translated 'confess' is *homologeo*, lit-erally 'to say the same thing'. The meaning of this word is clearly expressed in Psalm 51:4: 'Against you, you only, have I sinned and done what is evil in your sight, so that you are proved right when you speak and justified when you judge.' By confessing our sins, we are agreeing with God's verdict.

No interlude exists between confession and cleans-ing. 'If we confess our sins,' writes the apostle John, 'he is faithful and just and will forgive us our sins and purify us from all unrighteousness' (1 Jn 1:9). Brother Lawrence, whose experience of God has already been mentioned in this book, writes of the joy of forgive-ness and renewed fellowship with God:

> Touched by live repentance, I confess all my evil deeds to him; I implore his pardon, and give myself over into his hands to do with me as he will. This king, full of good-

ness and mercy, far from chastising me, embraces me lovingly, makes me eat at his table, serves me with his own hands, gives me the keys of his treasures and treats me just as if I were his favourite. He talks with me and has ceaseless pleasure in my company in a thousand thousand ways.[10]

These words are some of the most beautiful and happy that I have found in the writings of the great saints of the past. The Christian who understands the heart of his heavenly Father should not be pathologically obsessed with sin but overjoyed in God's forgiveness. All the pain and remorse associated with contrition and confession are merely the prelude to a blissful reconciliation to God.

Inability to accept God's forgiveness can be attributed to several factors. For the sake of directness, I will list these:

Ignorance of Scripture. Uncertainty about the scriptural teaching of forgiveness can result in insecurity. True repentance and confession result in forgiveness for all sins. Not only does God forgive, but he refuses to remember our sins (Heb 8:12).

The accusations of Satan. Satan is referred to as the accuser of the brethren (Rev 12:10–11). He delights in taking the Christian through the nightmare museum of his past sins, pointing out all the old trophies and relics, in an attempt to place him under condemnation. The only way to combat Satan is to talk back to him. 'They overcame him by the blood of the Lamb and by the word of their testimony,' writes John in Revelation. If our sins are hidden beneath the blood of Jesus, Satan has no right to make them public again. The blood of Jesus will strike dumb the devil and silence his accusations. Much of the guilt that Christians bear is the result of satanic harassment. The cross will tongue-tie the accuser.

Pride. Forgiven by Christ, there are those who cannot forgive themselves. At the root of this problem is pride. A person with self-knowledge will cry out with Paul, 'What a wretched man I am! Who will rescue me from this body of death?' (Rom 7:24). The realisation of our sinfulness will do more to sever the root of pride than any other experience. To face up to the fallenness of our nature is to accept that we are morally capable of any evil. Such a discovery will rid us of the smug, self-righteous complacency and superiority that can make the Christian so unattractive to others. Knowledge of sin kills the bigot and the Pharisee within us.

Restitution

Confession of sin has little reality if we are not prepared to make restitution for our deeds. After my own conversion, I had to return a number of stolen books to W.H. Smith. Confession was relatively easy, but restitution was an altogether more costly and humiliating business. Until I was prepared to be obedient to God in this matter, my books looked down upon me from their shelves like accusing faces. True confession brings restitution, reconciles people to one another and transforms attitudes and behaviour.

Soul friend

Confessing our sins to others is generally regarded by evangelicals as a Catholic practice. This view is not, in fact, an accurate record of Protestant thought. Luther and Malanchthon the Reformers, Richard Hooker and Jeremy Taylor the Puritans, and the Wesley brothers all advocated public confession. Moreover, their practice is not without a scriptural precedent. James writes in his Epistle: 'Therefore confess your sins to each other and pray for each other so that you may be healed. The prayer of a righteous man is powerful and effective' (Jas 5:16).

In the Celtic tradition of spirituality that gave birth to the English church, the 'soul friend' is an important figure. The soul friend is either a religious professional, ie, monk or priest, or a godly layperson. The qualities required of a soul friend are knowledge of Scripture and human nature, the ability to listen and keep confidences, and a gift for making the forgiveness of Christ real to the penitent. The rediscovery of the ministry of the soul friend could be of enormous benefit to the evangelical community.

Confessing one's sins to another can shatter the walls of isolation and secrecy and free the individual from prison. Confessing to God, in some cases, merely reinforces the feeling of secrecy that surrounds certain sins. To confess to a soul friend can disrupt the cycle of secrecy and guilt and lead to freedom from besetting sins. Openness about sin can be a therapy in itself. The process of confession, however embarrassing and painful, can allow another person to share our struggles and fight at our side in prayer.

The ministry of the confessional should not be distorted into the belief that we need to make public confession for every sin we commit. This makes a nonsense of the scriptural teaching that has already been explained in this chapter. The confessional is particularly advantageous to those who struggle with besetting sins or have been involved in sins that have left deep scars on the mind and spirit. In confessing our deepest struggles and moral failures to another human being, we allow an intrusion into our privacy. The door of the soul is flung wide and we invite a guest to enter.

At this point a clear warning must be given. The guest must be chosen carefully or great damage can be done. A friend of mine who confessed sins to another

Christian at a large conference became the subject of scandal. His 'guest' made his disclosures a matter of gossip. The choice of a soul friend, therefore, is very important, and to it we shall turn in the next chapter.

Confession is an important aspect of the devotional life. In a society that often makes virtues out of vices, the Christian can easily become desensitised to sin. A period of self-examination each day permits us to bring our sins to Christ for cleansing. If, however, there are certain sins and habits that constantly defeat us, access to a trusted soul friend can be a helpful therapy. This person need not be an elder or minister, but must be recognised as a person of integrity and wisdom.

Notes

1 Andrew Woolsey, *Duncan Campbell: A Biography* (Hodder and Stoughton and Faith Mission: London, 1974), p 118.

2 Morton T. Kelsey, *The Other Side of Silence* (SPCK: London, 1977), p 17.

3 Walter Eichdrodt, *Theology of the Old Testament*, vol 2 (SCM Press: London, 1967), p 270.

4 Rudolf Otto, *The Idea of the Holy* (Oxford University Press: London, 1980).

5 Richard Rolle, *The Fire of Love* (Penguin: London, 1972), p 69.

6 Richard Foster, *Celebration of Discipline* (Hodder and Stoughton: London, 1985), p 56.

7 T.S. Eliot, 'Burnt Norton, from *Four Quartets*', *Collected Poems* (Faber and Faber: London, 1963), p 190.

8 Sherwood Eliot Wirt (ed), *Spiritual Awakening* (Lion: Tring, 1986), p 190.

9 A.W. Tozer, *Paths to Power* (Christian Publications: Harrisburg, Pennsylvania), p 38.

10 Brother Lawrence, *The Practice of the Presence of God* (Hodder and Stoughton: London, 1987), p 45.

10

The Traveller and the Guide

'The basic premise of spiritual direction is that
in order to grow we need each other.'

Anne Long

In this chapter I intend to deal with the issue of guiding individuals towards spiritual maturity. In recent years, this subject has become a scorpion's nest of heresy and abuse. Indeed, in some churches, members are required to submit to their leaders and obey them in all things, but this approach to guidance cannot be encouraged; it will in most cases retard spiritual growth and result in infantilism. There is, however, a desperate need in the church for godly people who can guide others towards maturity.

Access to such people should not be obligatory but voluntary. We accept their advice and counsel because we want to. Such people are often referred to as 'spiritual directors' and those who seek their guidance as 'directees'. My comments about these terms are included later in the chapter, and I will retain their usage for the sake of clarity.

To most evangelicals, 'spiritual direction' signifies the general direction of the church, rather than the guidance of the individual. In this chapter, however, 'spiritual direction' refers to one-to-one or small group counselling.

The purpose of spiritual direction is twofold: to encourage the Christian to a more rewarding relation-

ship with God; and second, to enable the person to
relate his or her spirituality to life. A healthy spiritual
life will be expressed in consistent and godly living,
social and evangelistic concern, and peace and joy in
the Holy Spirit. The danger of metaphors like 'garden'
and 'secret room' (often used to describe the interior
life of the spirit) is that they can convey the impression of escapism. To meet God in secret is to live with
him in public.

In the history of the church, the director is variously
referred to as 'soul friend', 'spiritual father', 'spiritual
friend' or 'starets'. Within the Protestant tradition, the
pastor has often assumed the role of spiritual director.
Richard Baxter, writing in his classic, *The Reformed
Pastor*, recommends that five classes of people should
receive direction. These include non-Christians, those
who are struggling with sin, the backslidden, families,
and men and women who are living consistent Christian lives. This latter group is not ignored but are
counselled in order to make them even more fruitful in
the things of God. Baxter's pastoral theology is thus
not problem-centred. He suggests that the latter
group's counselling is specifically to encourage
development in their relationship with God.[1]

The ministries of pastoral care and spiritual direction are closely aligned. Gordon Jeff writes, 'It is difficult to make a clear-cut distinction between spiritual
direction and good pastoral care.'[2] Pastoral ministry
involves the dual function of counselling those with
special needs and problems, and directing the people
of God to a more satisfying and beautiful relationship
with him. The basic premise of spiritual direction is
therefore that in order to become mature in Christ we
need the assistance of others.

I begin by attempting to expose a weakness in the
church regarding spiritual direction, and conclude
with a number of practical suggestions. I have long

suspected that the role of spiritual director is crucial to the life and health of the church, though I am not enamoured with the title itself; 'spiritual director' is too formal for the majority of evangelical churches. The function is nevertheless crucially important. Perhaps the more biblical title of 'elder' would be a better description of the office. If we are to take relationship with God seriously, leaders must do all in their power to encourage the people of God to a healthy spirituality. Such a determination will not only involve excellent teaching but creative pastoral thinking, planning and organisation.

Lone Ranger or *Nineteen Eighty-four*?

Christianity is not a 'Lone Ranger' religion of rugged individualism; neither is it the religion of Orwell's novel, *Nineteen Eighty-four*, in which any form of individual initiative or expression is considered subversive. Both extremes, however, are evident in the church.

In some of the more recent discipling movements, there has been a tendency to subvert the individual to the will of selected leaders or to the Christian community at large. This can have the dual effect of stifling initiative and retarding spiritual growth. The most gifted sons and daughters of the church, from the apostle Paul onwards, have been distinguished by a certain degree of healthy individualism and even eccentricity. Rebels against the status quo, they were prepared to take enormous risks in the service of Christ and his kingdom.

The New Testament compares the church to a prism, and each believer to a facet of glass. When the light of God's Spirit falls on the prism, the shaft refracts, splintering into all the colours of the rainbow. The unity of the people of God transcends nationality, culture and gender, exhibiting to the 'rulers and authorities in the heavenly realms', the 'many coloured wisdom of God' (Eph 3:10).[3] To discourage a healthy individualism is to turn the prism opaque and its light into a dull, monotonous grey.

In more traditional churches the tendency is often quite the reverse. The church is viewed as a loose collection of individuals who like an ice flow in the Arctic Sea move in the same general direction, collide occasionally, but rarely grow together in warm personal relationships. In this caricature, the church is like a social club with certain rules and requirements of membership, but with no necessity for commitment and accountability. Excellent teaching can be given, but there is often no encouragement to the Christian to practise truth. The evangelical sermon with its high moral sentiments, exegetical purity and moments of light relief and entertainment is in danger of becoming a pious irrelevance, a weekly sedative administered by a religious professional. The model of the church is of a lecture theatre where students sit silently and listen, rather than a tutorial in which the people of God are encouraged to understand truth in order to apply it.

Anton Baumohl, in his timely book *Making Adult Disciples*, highlights this problem: 'Teaching methods used in the churches often leave the responsibility for application and action in the hands of individuals without attempting to help them.'[4] Anton's analysis reflects a lifetime of discipleship teaching and experience in the European church. His solution to the problem is a threefold pattern of leadership: the specialist who expounds the Scriptures; the enabler who works with small groups, encouraging participation and motivating to obedience; and the pastor/counsellor who deals with spiritual and emotional problems.

Roped together

Commenting on Ephesians 4:1–16, Professor Bruce said: 'The higher reaches of Christian life cannot be achieved in isolation from one's fellow believers.'[5] The passage in question refers to the importance of gifted leadership and the encouragement of fellow Christians if growth is to continue. To grow to maturity, 'attaining to the whole measure of the fulness of Christ', requires that 'each part [each member of the church] does its work' (Eph 4:13,16). In the Christian life, there should be no such thing as the solo climber. To scale the heights of spiritual experience demands that we be roped securely together with others. Some in the company will be gifted to lead, but their role will not be to dominate but to serve. The New Testament recognises the importance of godly and mature leadership but rejects the artificial divide between clergy and laity.

This distinction has done untold damage to the spiritual life of the church. Ministry, gifts, training— and to some extent, even spirituality—have been viewed as the exclusive preserve of a professional élite; amateurs are unwelcome. Fortunately, this distinction is slowly being broken down. The numerical weakness of the Western church has made it necessary to rethink the entire theology and practice of leadership. People are beginning to awake.

Church growth statistics substantiate the view that the church of the people is the church that grows. The truth of the priesthood of all believers deals the death blow to all forms of élitist and hierarchical leadership.

Eldership

One of the most interesting and significant developments in the modern church is the return to team leadership. In the New Testament, the spiritual care of the Christian was the responsibility of a leadership team referred to as elders and bishops. Scholars are generally agreed that the office of elder (*presbuteros*) and bishop (*episkopos*) are synonymous. In all probability, the concept of eldership was lifted from the Jewish synagogue. The word 'elder' denotes authority (Num 11:17; Deut 22:15; 25:7; 1 Kings 21:8; Mk 5:22; Acts 13:15). For those in the early church who were converted from a pagan background, the title 'bishop' (literally, 'overseer') would have been more meaningful. The word was used of magistrates, administrators, philosophers and moral and spiritual directors, signifying an important leadership role. The duties of the eldership include teaching and preaching (1 Tim 5:17), refuting false teaching (Acts 15:22–31), praying for the sick (Jas 5:14), recognising and authorising gifts (1 Tim 4:14), discipline (1 Tim 3:4–5), and spiritual direction and counselling (Acts 20:28; 1 Pet 5:3; Heb 13:17). The primary objective of leadership is to guide the people of God to spiritual maturity.

Within the evangelical tradition, churches have been experimenting with patterns of leadership for a number of years. Whether called 'elders', 'leaders', 'ministers' or 'priests', their function is often identical. The eldership is responsible for leading the church, teaching the Scriptures, pastoring the people, and exercising discipline when necessary. The weakness of the system, however, is in its offering little specialist guidance in the more subjective aspects of spirituality. Elders are often equipped to teach, pastor and counsel...but have little experience in directing the individual's private life with God. The cell group encourages participation and openness but is not necessarily the ideal context for spiritual direction. It is a rare individual who has been directed by a mature Christian in the ways of prayer, meditation, listening to God and the other disciplines of the interior life.

This, in my opinion, is one of the most disturbing weaknesses of modern evangelicalism. We can dress up our shallowness in happy choruses and fine words and sentiments, but there is often little depth or substance to our lives. Our spirituality can be a fairground spirituality of sensations, cheap thrills and excitement, but not much reality. It is difficult to discern the reasons for this malaise, but I would like to suggest four possibilities.

The Martha syndrome

The contemplative and active approaches to spirituality have often been compared to the two sisters, Mary and Martha. Mary was a contemplative, sitting at the feet of Jesus and listening to him, but Martha was an activist. Complaining to Jesus that her sister was not helping her with the housework, she was told that Mary had 'chosen what is better, and it will not be taken away from her' (Lk 10:41).

As evangelicals, we have a tendency to patronise Mary, condescendingly agreeing that she chose the better part, but secretly our sympathy is with Martha. We despise Mary's inactivity and by our attitudes and priorities endorse her sister's activism. The results of this activism are superficiality and emptiness of soul. Our theology is orthodox, our preaching correct; but the words that we utter can have a strange hollowness. Like an empty steel drum beaten with a hammer, we make a great deal of noise, but do not give the deep, resonant boom of full vessels. To talk of desire for God from an empty heart is like confessing love for one's wife or husband, when love has long since fled. The marriage is a sham, an empty formality. Both partners play their game, refer to each other as 'darling', and even deceive themselves; but the passion has gone, leaving only a ritual of words and actions. It is the measure of our blindness that when people come to our gatherings with a fierce desire for God, we do not always know how to cope with them; we feel embarrassed. Christianity without passion for God, however, is empty and meaningless.

Our unconscious priorities are often expressed in our public agenda. What we consider to be of supreme importance will be reflected in organisation, the educational programmes and the pastoral ministry of the church. Tragically, the devotional life of the congregation is often of secondary importance. Daily Bible notes are made available, and we pay lip service to the value of prayer, but encouragement to a full devotional life is generally neglected. Like Martha, we consider busyness more important than contemplation, public ministry of greater value than a private life with God. If you doubt the validity of my argument, attempt to answer the following questions:

—When did you last hear a series of messages on the devotional life?
—Who, in your local congregation, has been set aside to encourage and advise on the devotional life?
—Do you discuss the struggles and the joys of the devotional life in your cell/fellowship group?
—When you first became a Christian, were you taught how to benefit from Bible reading, meditation, study and Scripture memorisation? Were you given practical guidance in how to pray and listen to God?
—Has the impression ever been conveyed to you that the devotional life is of supreme importance?
—Are there books on the devotional life in your church library or book table? Are you encouraged to read them?

The private spirituality of the church is the true indication of a healthy public spirituality. It is easy to mistake lively preaching, an active and exciting programme, and demonstrative worship for a deep and real work of the Spirit. The real quality of the life and power of a church is determined by its membership. If the members have never been encouraged and directed to deepen their lives with God, there may be a measure of enthusiasm and a mild euphoria that passes for joy, but there will be little depth and genuine encounter with God.

The inhibited lover

Many people find it difficult to talk about their deepest feelings and longings. The devotional life is often seen as a private matter between ourselves and God; it is not something that we talk about to one another. The marriage symbolism of Scripture can also create a secrecy about our relationship with Christ. The Song of Songs, and many of the devotional writings of the church, refer to the relationship with God in explicitly intimate terms, using sexual imagery to express the wild intensity of the love of God and union with him; Christ and his bride are lovers who delight in each other. This parallel between husband and wife and Christ and his people can make the Christian reluctant to talk about the joys and difficulties of the spiritual life. Only an exhibitionist would discuss with another person his sexual exploits with his wife! In the relationship between ourselves and Christ, however, this secrecy can be damaging. A person's encounter with God is unique, but it is never exclusive. To live a healthy Christian life requires the advice and encouragement of others.

The intensely personal language of relationship with God is not the only reason for our silence. To admit to problems in our love-life with God can be as

embarrassing as admitting that one's marriage is not
as happy as it should be. Evangelicalism has a tendency to triumphalism. The God who reigns over the
universe and history can be too remote for the struggling Christian. Our acknowledgement of the tran-
scendence and power of God must be balanced by an
understanding of his immanence and humanity. In
the Person of Jesus, God wore our humanity, experienced our struggles and temptations, died in lonely
agony and exile, and rose again as our 'Great High
Priest' to cherish and care for us (Heb 2:10–18; 4:14–
16). Jesus is the human photograph of God. In him,
God recognises our vulnerabilities and weaknesses
and offers us grace and encouragement. In giving to us
a Great High Priest, God met us in our weakness. He
knew that we were vulnerable and needed help and
support. This view of God should be reflected in our
attitude to one another. As part of a priestly kingdom
under the supreme priesthood of Christ, we should be
open and honest with one another, supporting the
struggling, praying for them, and accepting them
without superiority or reserve. To tell the truth about
our deepest longings, fears and failures to another
brother or sister can be a remarkable therapy. Conversely, secrecy, and the fear associated with it can be
very damaging.

Hospital spirituality

The recent emphasis on counselling, emotional healing and therapy has sometimes overshadowed the
important ministry of spiritual direction. Thornton
refers to this obsession as the 'ambulance syndrome'.[6]
Counselling is seen primarily as a problem-solving
ministry. The Christian approaches the counsellor/
elder as a patient does a doctor. After a thorough
examination, the patient is diagnosed and the appropriate medicine is prescribed. The church becomes a

hospital for the casualties of life, not a training college for saints. Leaders can become so problem-centred that the success of a service is measured by public response. If a number of people approach them for problem-related counselling, they feel that the service has been successful.

Surely this is a false criterion for assessing success. Problem-related counselling certainly has its place in the church, but the primary task of leadership is to guide the people of God to spiritual maturity. During childhood, the slightest problem will bring the child running to his father or mother for help; but as the child matures, this happens less frequently. The child learns to handle the minor difficulties of life without needing constant parental support and encourage-ment. An overemphasis on problem-centred pastoral counselling can retard spiritual development and res-ult in a neurotic and self-preoccupied church.

The responsibility of leadership is not to create a church of spiritual hypochondriacs, but to point away from self to the glory of God. Admittedly, this will involve a certain amount of pastoral counselling and individual attention, but not to the exclusion of direct-ing the Christian to a more satisfying relationship with God. The New Testament church is not a hospital for chronically sick and disabled people, but a base camp from which we can climb the mountain of God.

The contemporary stress on honesty and problem-sharing is healthy and should be encouraged; but in some cases it can be an excuse for self-pity and atten-tion-seeking. Honesty about our problems is only commendable if we intend to do something about them. Leadership must attempt to put the character, courage and purpose back into God's people. To offer counsel and acceptance to those who have been damaged by life is crucial, but it should be part of the primary objective to present people mature in Christ

(Gal 4:19). This will undoubtedly involve the elder in a ministry of spiritual direction.

The penguin problem

The church has rarely been a creative institution. During times of revival, innovation and change have been more readily accepted, but this has not always been the case. John Wesley, for example, was driven out of the Church of England when he persisted in preaching the good news to the masses in the open air; Charles Finney, the great nineteenth-century revivalist, was attacked for his methods and theology of evangelism during the awakening in North America. So it is rare (but certainly not unknown) for people with a true pastoral ministry to be creative and visionary.

In fact, the nature of the ministry often inhibits daring and radical action. Committed to the people and their pastoral needs, leaders are often unprepared to take the kind of action that would disturb certain members of the flock. One can sympathise with this cautious approach. People are not laboratory guinea-pigs on which one can experiment; their feelings and longings must be taken into consideration. The role of the leader is gently, yet firmly, to guide the people of God, not to drive them with a whip. To move too slowly suggests a timid and frightened leadership, but to move too rapidly indicates insensitivity to people and the absence of wisdom. People are not pawns to be moved at will, but neither should their dogmatic and inflexible opinions impede the activity of the Spirit. The cantankerous and critical member can inadvertently hold up the work of God.

Timidity in leadership is often combined with the 'penguin problem'. Penguins rarely dive into the water unless one of their company has taken the plunge already. Once they are certain that the sea is free of marauders, they will spring noisily into the water. Similarly, leaders are often unwilling to adopt new ideas unless they have been tried out by other churches. Our pastoral theology and practice are rarely original. Risk-taking and courage are not the strong points of the Western church.

The absence of creative thought and originality has done much to retard spiritual growth. The New Testament church was pragmatic and creative, changing its structures to meet the needs of the people, but that kind of flexibility requires boldness and imagination among the leadership. One of the greatest needs of the modern church is spiritual direction and guidance for the people. It cries out to us from our congregations. Are we aware of the need? And if so, what are we doing about it?

With the recent interest in biblical spirituality, the idea of spiritual direction has become popular again. The role of director is adopted from monasticism. In the fourth century, a company of sincere Christians fled into the desert to escape the corruption and worldliness of the church. To avoid the deception that usually accompanies a personal quest for God and holiness, the novice was encouraged to find a spiritual father. Stephen Clark refers to these saintly and discerning individuals as 'unordained elders' who maintained 'both the health of the new movement and its good order within the Church'.[7] Since the desert movement, the spiritual father has always had an important function within monasticism. At his best, he has guided people to a more intimate relationship with God; at his worst, he has lacked imagination and sensitivity to the Holy Spirit, imposing a rigid system of spiritual discipline on the individual. Thomas Merton defines the role of spiritual director as 'God's usher',[8] describing his ministry as that of leading 'souls in God's way'.[9] As men and women of spiritual wisdom and discernment, their task is to guide us 'to see and obey our real director—the Holy Spirit'.[10]

A number of books have been written on spiritual direction, the majority of them by non-evangelicals, and little attempt has been made to make the ministry of direction viable in the church as a whole. One notable exception is Gordon Jeff's sensible and practical book, *Spiritual Direction for Every Christian*.[11] Martin Thornton's *Spiritual Direction* (subtitled 'A Practical Introduction') contains some interesting material, but to refer to it as practical is to lose sight of reality altogether!

Within the evangelical community, there is a growing awareness of the importance of proper spiritual direction. Originally, the idea of spiritual direction was monastic; it therefore requires reinterpretation if it is to be viable in an evangelical context. The need for direction is evident, but how to meet that need is a difficult and demanding question. The practical suggestions that I make in the latter part of this chapter are merely signposts, ideas that can be discussed and developed in the local church.

The qualities of a spiritual director

Warmth

The spiritual director must never be a remote, dispassionate individual. There is almost unanimous agreement by modern writers on the subject that the director should be warm and personable. Gordon Jeff advises the director to establish a relationship with the directee as quickly as possible. The director must have the ability to open himself and share from his experience without being self-assertive. Such openness should encourage an identical response from the directee.[12]

Spiritual direction, therefore, is not an élitist ministry. The director and directee are fellow travellers walking towards the same destination. The director has the advantage of maturity and experience, but this does not imply superiority. He is qualified to warn his companion of the dangers of the road and advise on the best possible route. Aware of his companion's capabilities, he provides an itinerary of travel that will motivate without discouraging him because of its difficulties. The relationship between them both is not the formal relationship of a doctor with a patient, or a manager with an interviewee, but the camaraderie of friends who share a common purpose.

Spirituality and maturity

The director need not be a spiritual superman or superwoman, but anyone who aspires to the office must be consistent and mature. A theorist may be useful in a classroom, but spiritual direction implies practical experience. To encourage another to pray, meditate and listen to God without practical experience is rather like a bachelor giving advice on marriage. Textbooks may be consulted, the advice may be useful, but there will be no practical basis for his remarks. Moreover, it is useful for the director himself or herself to have access to a spiritual director. No Christian, however godly or mature, will reach a state of perfection where input from others will become unnecessary.

Discernment

Some people are naturally discerning and shrewd, whereas others have a more trusting nature. The director needs to see beyond the psychological smokescreens of the directee and discern the real person. Moreover, he should be sufficiently sensitive to the Holy Spirit to perceive the work of God in the directee's life.

For those who are not naturally perceptive, a measure of discernment can be developed through experience and prayer. Strangely enough, some people can be frightened by perceptive directors. The uncanny ability to read the other person can be interpreted as a violation of privacy. In such cases, the director must consciously hold back, allowing the directee to volunteer information in his own time. The gift of 'X ray' vision is immensely useful, but not everyone likes the idea of being naked before their director. If God gives the gift of discernment, it must be used with tact and wisdom.

Knowledge

A knowledge of Christian theology and Scripture is essential in spiritual direction. Without proper training, approaches to prayer and the other aspects of the inner life can be individualistic and unimaginative. Exposure to other traditions of spirituality can add depth and variety to the interior life.

If it is decided that a system of spiritual direction will be of benefit to your church, it may be practical to give the directors a basic training. This may be given by the pastor/vicar, or a specialist can be invited for the purpose. The training programme can also include a recommended book list.

To avoid isolationism, the directors should be encouraged to meet together regularly. On these occasions, they can pray together, exchange ideas, and share their experience of God. These times can also be used to advance the education of spiritual directors. A series of lectures on Christian spirituality can be given, providing useful input. The director, like the directee, is a learner. He is not the sole possessor of specialist knowledge, but a person whose own relationship with God is still developing. Each day brings new discoveries and surprises.

Confidentiality and the ability to listen

The director must find the balance between listening and giving advice. Henri Nouwen refers to his director, John Eudes, in his celebrated *Genesee Diary*. John seems to have found the right balance between listening and making insightful comment:

> He gave me much time and attention, but did not allow me to waste a minute; he left me fully free to express my feelings and thoughts, but did not hesitate to present his own; he offered me space to deliberate about choices and to make decisions, but did not withhold his opinion that some choices were better than others; he let me find my own way, but did not hide the map that showed the right direction. In our conversation, John Eudes emerged not only as a listener, but also as a guide, not only as a counsellor, but also as a director.[13]

The ability to know when to listen and when to speak can only be learned by experience. To give another human being our complete, undivided attention is a great compliment. Often we are so obsessed with ourselves and our own ideas and opinions that we find it impossible to listen. We may be silent; our face may wear a suitable expression of sympathy and concern, but our attention is elsewhere. Our selfish ego can be so subtle that we are unable to detect its presence. Our inability to give another person our total attention may be a symptom of a deep spiritual disorder. Their opinions and desires are considered unimportant in comparison to our own. The spiritual director must have the ability to listen, to hear the words of the directee and the subtle inflections of feelings and longing that they convey.

A good director will always be a listener, but his ministry does not end here. Spiritual direction, as the title suggests, implies guidance. John Eudes was undoubtedly an excellent listener, but he was not

afraid to offer clear and decisive guidance when
necessary. The guidance may only involve a few sentences, or it may constitute a long discourse.

It should go without saying that confidentiality is
crucial to spiritual direction. Things said in secret
should not be shouted from the roof top. A person will
never be frank and open about the mysteries of his
heart if he thinks that they'll become the subject of
local gossip.

The election of spiritual directors

The church is not generally good at identifying men
and women of God. The leaders of the local church are
often those who are more conspicuous, powerful and
articulate. The meek may inherit the earth, but they
don't fare so well in the church. In fact, deeply spiritual people are often considered slightly eccentric or
fanatical. Public gifts are easy to recognise, but the
more secret disciplines of prayer, meditation, silence
and worship are, by their very nature, hidden from
public view. A secret life with God, however, is usually difficult to keep hidden. A person who is intimate
with God in secret will be unable to disguise that
intimacy in public. There will be little ostentation and
show, but the Christian will demonstrate an ardour
and passion for God that is impossible to conceal.

There are three ways by which spiritual directors
can be identified:

Selection by discernment
Through prayer, leaders discern the spiritual people
among their members and commission them as directors. The leaders themselves can be included as spiritual directors.

Selection by volunteering

In this approach, leaders invite people to volunteer as spiritual directors. Inevitably, this will be an untidy process. A number who respond may be totally unsuitable, and many who have the necessary qualities will be too self-effacing to respond.

Selection by investigation

A questionnaire, similar to the one that provided the practical information for this book (p 221), can be used. This can be given to the leaders and members of the local church. No pressure should be placed on anyone to fill it in. The response must be voluntary, but there is no harm in mentioning how useful the information will be.

If the majority of church members fill in the questionnaire, it will have a dual effect: the secret spiritual life of the church will be exposed, and potential spiritual directors will be identified. It is important to reassure everyone that the elders/leaders are not turning into a power-crazy secret police with undertones of 'Big Brother Is Watching You'. To avoid the 'them' and 'us' syndrome, it must also be made clear that the leaders themselves are completing the questionnaire.

The difficulty of any selection process is the basic assumption that leaders are more spiritually mature than the congregation. This is not always the case. The leaders may be theologically trained and have a more 'sophisticated' understanding of spiritual life, but they may lack the spiritual stature of many rank-and-file church members. Such a discovery need not be harmful. An insecure leader may masquerade as a man of God, concealing his inner poverty and struggles from other members of the church. Afraid of disqualification as a leader, he can become increasingly isolated. Conversely, a secure leader will happily recognise and endorse those of his congregation who are his spiritual superiors. He may even submit to the spiritual direction of someone in his own congregation.

We must never underestimate the importance of scriptural and theological study, but they do not in themselves imply a rich devotional life with God. Leaders may be in danger of teaching their people without practising themselves. Theology is to be lived as well as taught. This may seem like a cliché, but it is crucially important to the life of the church. The pulpit, if we are not careful, can be used as an escape from the realities of life, a symbol of our irrelevance and impotence. Surrounded by the mystique of the professional ministry, we hide our emptiness in a welter of words and sermonising.

Jesus and the apostle Paul encouraged imitation (Mk 3:14; 1 Cor 4:17; 2 Tim 3:10). Much of the teaching of Jesus was not of the formal variety—the Sabbath sermon—but was the spontaneous response to questions. 'One day Jesus was praying in a certain place,' writes Luke. 'When he had finished, one of his disciples said to him, "Lord, teach us to pray, just as John taught his disciples" ' (Lk 11:1). The Lord's life was open to public scrutiny. He taught his disciples by example and word. His life gave his teaching authority. The need of our time is not necessarily for great thinkers or communicators, but great saints. The deeply lined, yet somehow beautiful, compassionate face of Mother Teresa of Calcutta is a far more evocative portrait of spiritual greatness than the studious, self-assured image of Western clergy. Quietly to live the life of Jesus on earth is the most powerful sermon of all.

The dangers of spiritual direction

Authoritarianism

Martin Thornton refers to spiritual direction as a 'mutual quest rather than an authoritarian discipline'.[14] An authoritarian approach to spiritual direction can be damaging. The finest directors are those who see themselves as servants, since the purpose of direction is not to impose a rigid system of spiritual behaviour on the directee, but quietly to encourage a deeper relationship with God. The spiritual director's role is comparable to that of a driving instructor. The instructor gives practical advice on driving skills and criticises defective technique. His intention is not to dominate the learner, but impart the training which will enable the learner to pass the driving test and use a car safely. Similarly, the spiritual director's job is to encourage the directee towards maturity. His role is not to make himself indispensable, but like the instructor, to impart the training that will ultimately make him redundant. Once the instruction has been given and acted upon, he may maintain a loose relationship with the directee, but his major function is over.

An authoritarian director will retard spiritual growth and encourage dependency. Gordon Jeff perceptively points out that 'directors are to be used as signposts rather than props'.[15] One of the dangers of such insecurity in a director is that it results in and stems from a desire to dominate other people. By imposing his will on others, the insecure director feeds a crippled, parasitic ego with harmful consequences. As a spiritual father, he refuses to allow his children to grow up.

Uniformity

Relationship with God cannot be defined by a formula. A six-point plan for relationship with God may contain some useful hints, but it can never do justice to its depth and variety. Several Christian organisations have produced helpful information and material to encourage prayer, meditation, study and the memorisation of Scripture. In some cases, the material is used in conjunction with a one-to-one or a group discipleship programme. There are certainly benefits with this approach, but there is one serious danger. The development of the spiritual life does not work like an assembly line. To expect each individual to conform to an identical programme is to overlook the complexity of human nature and the mystery of relationship with God, of the Spirit's work in individual lives. The best kind of spiritual director is able to read human nature and discern the work of the Spirit in the person's life. Indeed, Thomas Merton insists that 'no amount of theological study can give a man spiritual discernment'.[16] A codified spirituality, although better than nothing, is a poor substitute for proper spiritual direction.

Subjectivism

Another potential danger of spiritual direction is an unhealthy subjectivism. The director can be so intent on the subjective aspects of spirituality that the Scriptures are neglected altogether. To avoid deception and fantasy, spiritual experience must be referred constantly to the word of God. To encourage prayer without reference to the Bible is like planting grass seed in concrete. The Scriptures are definitive in the interpretation of experience. The word must interpret experience, and not experience the word.

One Christian director known to me advises those she is directing to read and meditate on the relevant passages of Scripture. If, for example, she wishes to encourage a more Christ-centred spirituality, she will ask the directee to study the passages of Scripture that relate to the subject. She may also recommend other reading material. The advantage of this approach is that all experience is determined and tested by Scripture.

The spiritual life is a journey beset with many dangers. To attempt the journey without a map, compass and an experienced guide can be fatal. The map and compass represent the Scriptures; the guide is the witness and direction of the church. We need both if we are to negotiate the dangers and snares of the road.

The setting for spiritual direction

The more relaxed and informal the setting for spiritual direction, the better the response should be. Admittedly, there are rare individuals who prefer a more formal context, eg, a minister's study, but such people are in the minority. A comfortable lounge with armchairs is preferable to the white-walled austerity of a vestry or study.

There is a danger in being super-spiritual about direction. Providing the Spirit is present, we say direction will be successful—and of course it will—but it would be unwise to overlook the importance of surroundings. Restaurant owners often have a better grasp of human psychology than church leaders! A warm, inviting atmosphere, tasteful but not intrusive decor and soft lighting can contribute as much to the success of an evening as the quality of the cuisine. In a restaurant, the attractive, unthreatening atmosphere permits easy and intimate conversation. Similarly, comfortable and inviting surroundings, especially in the one-to-one relationship, are conducive to relaxation and openness.

The director should avoid sitting behind a desk, or adopting any position of superiority. 'Spiritual direction,' writes Thornton, 'spells two amateurs and no desk and no couch.'[17] The need to assume a position of superiority is a disturbing trait in a director's character. If the director's ego demands a desk behind which to sit, or a chair from which he can pontificate and look down at the directee, an insecurity is already beginning to appear in his temperament which may disqualify him from office. Aelred of Rievaulx, one of the great directors of the past, prayed, 'You know, Lord, my intention is not so much to be their superior as to lovingly help them and humbly serve them, to be at their side, one of them.'[18] This prayer should be on the lips of any would-be spiritual directors. The task of the director is to come alongside, to serve, to encourage, and not to play the power game of 'great guru' who condescends to offer advice to a weaker brother or sister.

The regularity of spiritual direction

The frequency of spiritual direction will depend upon the particular needs of the directee. Here one might draw a parallel between the development of a new aircraft and the formation of the spiritual life. During the development stage, regular testing is necessary to ascertain reliability and performance. Before a new aeroplane can be sold to airline companies, the prototype is exhaustively tested. This process, however, does not cease with its production. The testing is not so frequent, but it continues all the same. If a fault is detected, even in only one aircraft, the entire fleet is often grounded for inspection. Regular service guarantees the longevity of the aircraft and the safety of passengers.

The initial period of spiritual direction compares to

the experimental stage of aircraft development. No fixed period can be given for this formative time in a person's spiritual development. The length of the time will be determined by need, not by any programme. To provide continuity, it is advisable to meet once every one or two weeks. Several sessions should be spent establishing rapport. It may become obvious during this time that director and directee are not suited. This should not cause alarm. Human personality is so complex that however gifted and able a director, he will not be able to handle every kind of temperament. If this is the case, the director should find the directee a new director rather than waste time or cause hurt trying to make the relationship work.

The difference between spiritual direction and the evangelical discipling process is that the former allows the spiritual needs of the person to determine the guidance given. Spiritual direction is a person-centred ministry. By contrast, the discipling process often relies on a Bible study course or programme. These approaches have an equal validity and importance: in the first, the subjective aspects of spirituality are encouraged; in the second, a consistent programme of teaching about the Christian faith is given to stimulate practical spirituality. Undoubtedly there is a significant overlap, but spiritual direction and discipling are basically different in nature and purpose. Though they are both included in the wider meaning of Christian discipleship, they constitute different emphases. Let me illustrate with an imaginary situation.

The director and directee sit in a warm, comfortable lounge. Both are noticeably relaxed. The formalities are over, rapport is established, and they can now get down to business. The directee starts talking naturally, without any sign of embarrassment. God is remote to her, she confesses, hardly the Father-figure envisaged in the Bible. The director listens attentively,

signifying by the occasional nod of the head or brief
question that she understands. The apparent aloof-
ness of God, says the directee, is making prayer difficult.

Rather than giving a lecture on the fatherhood of
God, the director then asks about the directee's parents. She learns that the father has always been austere and remote, rarely showing warmth or affection
towards the family. Her concept of fatherhood has
been derived from her human father. Turning to
Scripture, the director attempts to show that God's
fatherhood is loving and intimate.

After an hour and a half, the session concludes. The
director suggests to her directee that she should meditate on the passages in the Bible that relate directly to
the fatherhood of God. She also suggests that she
reflect on the Scriptures that refer to God as 'Husband', 'Bridegroom', 'Friend', and 'Shepherd'. These
will encourage a more positive and loving picture of
God. If she still feels that God is distant, the Gospels
can provide an effective antidote. In Jesus, God
becomes personal and human. He takes our humanity
and wears it comfortably, touches us with human
hands and smiles with a human face. In Jesus, God
crosses the immeasurable distance between himself
and man and takes his place beside us.

This may be an idealised picture of spiritual direction, but it does give some idea of the nature and
scope of the ministry, distinguishing it from the familiar Bible study approach.

Once the directee is established in the disciplines of
the spiritual life, the need for frequent and intense
spiritual direction is no longer necessary. The directee, however, must not be abandoned altogether. At
regular intervals, the directee should meet with his
spiritual director. There are two reasons for this. First,
to meet our spiritual director involves accountability.

If, for example, we have been undisciplined or self-indulgent in our prayer-life, his questions will quickly expose us. Second, the spiritual director can give fresh input and correct any imbalance or self-deception. Self-knowledge is not easy to come by. The Holy Spirit can impart moments of brilliant clarity in which our true self stands naked and exposed; but much of the time, our perception of self is like looking at our reflection in a broken mirror. The image that stares back at us is often distorted and fragmentary, shattered into tiny pieces by both our illusions and our low self-esteem. A director who has truly studied our inner landscape and is familiar with its contours will often have an objectivity that we lack. She or he can apply both the scalpel and the salve.

I am aware that the word 'accountability' has the wrong connotion in some Christian circles, conveying the idea of an uncritical submission to leadership. The accountability that is mentioned here is voluntary. There is nothing sinister or manipulative about it. In fact, without accountability, life would quickly degenerate into chaos. Accountability provides the incentive for excellence. In sport, the skills of an athlete are honed by his coach. If the coach detects a reluctance to train or a poor mental attitude, he will challenge the athlete and demand improvements. Similarly, accountability to a spiritual director can provide the impetus for a godly life of worship and service. To disregard any kind of accountability will not enhance our spirituality but destroy it.

It is difficult to say how much time should be given to each session. In fact, most of us are unable to concentrate for long. Moreover, if direction is given in the evening, time is limited. An hour and a half to two hours is usually sufficient for a session, but this can be extended in an emergency.

After the formative period of direction is over, the

directee may see the director every two or three
months. In time, the gaps between these sessions will
grow longer as the directee matures in Christ.

For would-be directors who read this chapter, the
qualifications of spiritual direction may seem unat-
tainable. A trainee director, however, does not need
all the qualities mentioned in this chapter, but must
be willing to learn. Providing there is a humility and
sincere desire to learn, his or her ministry will probably be effective. Of course, in the early days of the
ministry, mistakes will be made, but these do not
disqualify from office. Mistakes can often be of greater
benefit than successes, a wealth of experience sal-
vaged from a failure.

Although I have used the masculine gender in this
chapter more often than the feminine to describe the
spiritual director, this has been done in the interests
of style, rather than from any sexist standpoint. Of
course, both men and women qualify. Commonsense
should determine which director is used with a particular directee. There are certain dangers associated
with being directed by a member of the opposite sex.
Strong sexual and emotional attraction can occur, or
there may even be a reluctance on the part of the
directee to share intimately about herself/himself.
Many men and women have successfully directed
members of the opposite sex, but we would be silly to
ignore the dangers. As a general rule, an older man or
woman can safely direct a younger person of the
opposite sex, but even so, the risk of entanglement is
not removed altogether. I hesitate to recommend that
the director and directee should always be of the same
sex, but I must give a clear warning of possible difficulties.

Spiritual friends

I have dealt with a very specialist form of spiritual
direction, but this chapter would be incomplete without mentioning other forms of direction. The early
Methodists practised direction in their band meet-
ings. The leader would closely question each member
of the small band group and then give advice on the
spiritual life. Public confession of sin and honesty
about the condition of one's heart were encouraged.

The danger of small group direction is twofold:
highly vocal or very needy people can constantly grab
the limelight, excluding less forthcoming members
from the benefits of spiritual direction; second, group
direction does not permit the kind of individual guidance envisaged in one-to-one direction. On the other
hand, group direction can act as a check to eccentric
and misguided counsel. Silly or dangerous advice can
be modified by the wisdom of more discerning
people. A spiritual director is inevitably limited by his
tradition of churchmanship and experience. But the
advantage of the group is that it permits each member
to share from his or her experience. The dangers of
being directed by a member of the opposite sex have
already been mentioned. In group direction these
problems are largely overcome. The group can benefit
from the extraordinary richness of male *and* female
approaches to spirituality.

Informal direction can go on within the context of
marriage. A husband and wife should encourage each
other spiritually. The argument that they are not sufficiently dispassionate to have the objectivity necessary for direction can be a fallacy. It seems
inconceivable that lovers who know the other's body
and mind with the intimacy of long familiarity should
be incapable of understanding the soul of their partner. Ideally, marriage should be the most intense and
real of all human relationships. The nudity of married

lovers should become the emotional and spiritual nakedness of two people who no longer need to pretend. The one flesh union is not only the twinning of bodies but also souls.

I can anticipate the obvious criticisms of this view. Here we have the ideal of marriage, but reality often falls far short of it. A couple can make love, parent children, socialise and enjoy one another's company, but have nothing in common spiritually. At the deepest level of their existence, they repel rather than attract. To discuss the spiritual life and pray together is almost impossible. The husband and wife speak a different spiritual language. They are not the soul mates God intends them to be. Such a problem requires specialist counselling.

A disparity in spiritual maturity can also create tension within a marriage. In such a relationship, the strong partner either assumes responsibility for the weaker, or becomes frustrated with his or her spiritual progress. In either case, a problem emerges. If the husband or wife constantly carries the partner, the marriage will lack reciprocity. One partner does most of the giving, while the other passively receives. If, on the other hand, the stronger partner becomes impatient with the spiritual progress of his or her mate, the result can be polarisation. The less mature member of the duo is made to feel inadequate by the impatience of the partner. That kind of pressure retards growth rather than encouraging it.

In a more balanced marriage, where husband and wife are of similar maturity, informal direction should be encouraged. This can happen spontaneously or can be organised in advance. A husband and wife who have taken their relationship with each other and God seriously should be familiar with the geography of the other's soul. In the intimacy of marriage, they are tuned to each other's moods with the innate sensitivity of a predator to the scent of its prey!

This informal direction does not exclude the direction of someone outside the family. The devotional life of a couple can be restricted by their own experience of God. Access together to a godly director can enhance the quality and depth of their spiritual life.

Spiritual friendship also provides a means of informal spiritual direction. A spiritual friendship is a relationship which gives the spiritual dimension of life priority. The individual opens his heart to his friend, allowing another brother or sister to share the yearnings and longings of his soul. Spiritual friends often make themselves accountable to one another, encouraging or gently rebuking when the occasions arise.

While discipleship programmes serve a useful purpose, specialist spiritual direction offers the best kind of guidance for the more subjective aspects of spirituality. But spiritual friendship is a worthwhile alternative when this ministry is unavailable. Even when access to a godly director is possible, spiritual friendship can still be extremely profitable. To pray, to share, to study with another person can be a tremendous incentive to spiritual growth.

The suggestions in this chapter are no more radical than the training programmes of the secular world. Doctors, engineers, plumbers, teachers, biologists, mechanics and bus drivers all require adequate training. Who would like to be driven by a bus driver who had not received a proper road training? The answer to this question is obvious. Why, then, are we so reluctant to give Christians the training that they need to be men and women of God? The institutional church is one of the most ancient establishments on earth, but it can also be among the most amateur and short-sighted. Christ's command to make disciples of all nations not only included the sacrament of baptism, but training and teaching in the Christian life (Mt 28:16–20).

The call of this chapter for spiritual directors is a response to the desperate need of the people of God. If my suggestions are dismissed as untenable or impractical, what better alternative can you provide to deepen the spiritual life of the church? The destiny of all God's children is to enjoy and love him for ever. A church strategy that does not reflect this priority and actively encourage deep communion with God could well be missing out on his purpose.

Notes

1 See Richard Baxter, *The Reformed Pastor* (Banner of Truth: Edinburgh, 1974).

2 Gordon Jeff, *Spiritual Direction for Every Christian* (SPCK: London, 1987), p 25.

3 The Greek adjective *polypoikilos* is translated 'manifold' in most versions of the Bible. The literal translation is 'many-coloured'.

4 Anton Baumohl, *Making Adult Disciples* (Scripture Union: London, 1984), p 24.

5 F.F. Bruce, *The Epistle to the Ephesians* (Pickering and Inglis: Glasgow, 1961), p 87.

6 Martin Thornton, *Spiritual Direction* (SPCK: London, 1984), p 9.

7 Stephen Clark, *Unordained Elders and Renewed Communities* (Paulist Press: New York, 1976), p 48.

8 Thomas Merton, *Spiritual Direction and Meditation* (Anthony Clarke Books: Wheathampstead, 1975), p 20.

9 *Ibid*, p 20.

10 *Ibid*, p 33.

11 Jeff, *op cit*.

12 *Ibid*, p 13.

13 Henri Nouwen, *The Genesee Diary* (Image Books: New York, 1981), p 15.
14 Thornton, *op cit*, p 126.
15 Jeff, *op cit*, p 17.
16 Thomas Merton, *Contemplative Prayer* (Darton, Longman and Todd: London, 1968), p 135.
17 Thornton, *op cit*, p 126.
18 Cited in Kenneth Leech, *Soul Friend* (Sheldon Press: London, 1977), pp 53–54.

11

Some Detours on the Journey

'I hold that devotion to Jesus Christ separates us from the world and its sins as well as identifies us with the world in its suffering.'

Donald Bloesch

Cheap grace

A defective understanding of conversion can seriously impair our enjoyment of God. The custom among some evangelicals to take people through a predictable sequence of steps and then ask them to make a short prayer of commitment, while useful, has potential dangers. Conversion can be reduced to an impersonal assembly-line technique. Such a hurried approach was certainly not encouraged by early Protestant teachers. Even a quick reading of books from the Reformers, the Puritans, the Pietists and other post-Reformation groups reveals a very serious and enlightened view of conversion to Christ. Johann Arndt, the Lutheran mystic, writes, 'Truly, to be born of God is not a transient shadow, or an empty name without reality. It must needs be a lively and powerful production, and something that becomes [ie, gives honour to] the majesty of almighty God.'[1] To help another towards faith in Christ is spiritual midwifery, not a form of cheap salesmanship. To rush the process, to refuse to listen and probe, to be insensitive to the guidance of the Holy Spirit can result in spurious conversions. Still-births remain one of the greatest tragedies of modern evangelism. True conversion involves a life-changing encounter with the living God.

Evangelical teaching rightly insists on the importance of salvation by grace. Unfortunately, however, the church has often tried either to turn the grace of God into a legal system of merit or reward, or else a morally neutral doctrine of cheap grace.

Grace is God's extravagant generosity towards a disobedient, undeserving and sinful people. This grace, however, must never be caricatured as coming from the free gift department of the kingdom of heaven—as if God generously bestows forgiveness, sonship, the Holy Spirit and the certainty of heaven without the necessity of accountability and obedience. To subscribe to such a view is to turn God into a benevolent Father Christmas, a morally undemanding Deity who is content to be patronised provided we visit his store and pay him token loyalty.

The impact of this erroneous concept of grace has been disastrous. To become a Christian thus is no more costly than filling in a form with the appropriate responses, or receiving a gift from a cereal packet. In this parody, salvation by grace is merely a rational, utilitarian process whereby God does all the giving and the believer passively receives. The gospel is floated on the Stock Exchange; conversion is consumerised. God no longer encounters the individual and humbles his pride, but nervously negotiates a business deal for his soul. If the terms are unsatisfactory, man casually rejects his Creator.

The temptation to cheapen the grace of God has always been evident in the church. The Puritan preacher Thomas Watson quaintly draws attention to the fact: 'He who sells cheapest shall have the most customers; the Devil knows that it is a cheap and easy doctrine which pleases the flesh, and he doubts not but he shall have customers enough.'[2] These words should sober us and recall us to reality. To compromise the integrity of the gospel in an attempt to attract converts can be the devil's work. The message of the grace of God is not a little bit of religious sentimentality, but the declaration of God's loathing for sin and his passionate, suffering love for mankind. Grace may be free but it is never cheap. Grace leaves the splendour of heaven for a manger in Bethlehem; suffers hunger and thirst and all the other limitations of humankind; experiences loneliness, rejection and sorrow, and finally submits to a criminal's death in order to win a rebel world. In the Christian gospel, grace is given a human face: the face of Jesus of Nazareth (2 Cor 8:9).

The doctrine of grace is virtually meaningless until someone is struck down by the holy lightning of God's presence and sees the warped landscape of his own heart. The parable of the tax collector and the Pharisee (Lk 18:9–14) brilliantly illustrates this truth. The Pharisee is so obsessed with his own righteousness that the grace of God is irrelevant. To suggest to the Pharisee that he is incapable of pleasing God is both to insult his pride and nullify a lifetime of strict religious observance. The tax collector, on the other hand, is shattered by the discovery of his moral ineptitude and cries to God for mercy: 'God, have mercy on me, a sinner.' At the very moment when the tax collector feels least godlike, he is seized by grace, forgiven of sin and welcomed into the family of God. Paradoxically, the discovery of infinite distance from God results in the most dramatic experience of his proximity: he enters the temple an enemy of God and leaves as his friend.

Grace is always a poison to the pride of man, but to those who have discovered their own sinfulness, it is a medicine that brings healing and life. The true nature of grace only becomes apparent when we see ourselves in the blaze of God's holiness. This realisation need not be an experience of a moment, but the culmination of a painful process of self-discovery. The end result, however, is always the same: the humbling and liberating truth that all our moral endeavour and religiosity is not sufficient to win the approval of God. We approach God not on the basis of what we have done for him, but rather on the basis of what he has done for us. Grace, in essence, is God's initiative on our behalf: seeing us guilty, he cancels our criminal record; seeing us imprisoned, he frees us; seeing us helpless, he imparts strength by his Holy Spirit; seeing us orphaned, he adopts us. Grace gives boundlessly and joyfully, yet demands from us an equivalent response. Grace frees us from sin in order that we might serve and obey God.

To envisage conversion without a radical change of behaviour is then as unthinkable as splitting the atom without precipitating a nuclear reaction. Grace has made us new creations in Christ. If the new creation continues to act and behave as the old, we are justified in concluding that there is something seriously amiss.

The doctrine of grace is not always easy for Westerners to understand. We are educated from childhood to see reward as the result of labour. Grace is the antithesis of this principle, hence the dichotomy in the New Testament of grace and works (Rom 3:27–31; Gal 2:15–21; 3:1–14). So inculcated in our minds is this idea of 'work brings reward', however, that it can unconsciously influence our relationship with God. For the Christian who has never fully understood grace, there will always be a tendency to guilt-inspired activism. Some of the most beautifully expressed writings of the church have been written by men and women who were confused at this point.

Many of the excesses of the early and medieval mystics can only be understood in this context. Bereft of a proper understanding of grace, the Christian will always attempt to extenuate his guilt and buy God's favour with the worthless currency of works. The greater the disquiet of conscience, the more extreme will be the penance, asceticism and labour. Grace drives the guilt and anxiety from the human heart, allowing the Christian to relax in the company of God.

If grace is defined as God's generous initiative on our behalf, the human response to grace is faith. John Stott describes faith as 'the eye that looks to Christ, the hand that lays hold of him, the mouth that drinks the water of life'.[3] There is nothing magical about this quality; it is simply an attitude of humble, adoring trust in God. Grace gives and faith receives with open hands. There is an enormous difference, however, between the biblical doctrine of faith and the 'easy believism' of much modern evangelicalism. The reverse side of faith is obedience. 'Only he who believes is obedient,' cries Bonhoeffer, 'and only he who is obedient believes.'[4] Faith and obedience are so closely related in the New Testament that they cannot be divorced from one another without serious consequence (Jn 3:36; Rom 1:5; 1 Pet 1:2; Jas 2:26). To have faith in God results in a life of obedience to him. A faith that does not find expression in good works is spurious.

Quick-fit spirituality

If 'cheap grace' describes an inadequate theology of conversion, the aphorism 'easy grace' refers to an inadequate view of sanctification. To maintain a consistent devotional life, discipline is crucial. It is here, however, that Western Christianity is weak. In recent years a disciplined devotional life has been discouraged. Writing in the compendium *The Study of Spirituality*, Edward Yarnold documents this trend. The reluctance to rise early for private prayer, he argues, 'is indicative of a loss of faith not so much in the value of prayer as in the value of discipline for all areas of life'.[5]

There are several reasons for this neglect. The first relates to the attitude which I have described as 'easy grace'. 'I'm no longer under law but grace, brother!' is often said in defence of a spiritual lifestyle that would have us sacked from any secular job. A stress on time management, rising early for prayer, regular Bible study and meditation is described as legalism. To endorse such behaviour (some say) is to submit to the bondage of the law. Grace and discipline are seen as contrary to one another. Such a view of grace, however, is clearly unscriptural. In fact, so important is discipline that we will all be accountable to Christ at his judgement seat 'for the things done while in the body, whether good or bad' (2 Cor 5:10). Grace, therefore, is not an excuse for laziness and indiscipline, but the dynamism for a life of self-sacrifice and toil. To enjoy God requires a disciplined devotional life. If we fail here, our experience of God will be erratic and unsatisfactory.

The 'easy grace' theology has an even more subtle influence on our thinking than the abandonment of a life of discipline. A defective doctrine of grace can turn our heavenly Father into an indulgent parent. He fondly overlooks the weaknesses of his children, responding immediately to every demand that is made upon him. This 'quick-fit' style of spirituality is highly dangerous. God loves us far too deeply to spoil us. He longs for intimacy with us but is also determined to sculpt the stubborn rock of human character into the likeness of his Son. The journey into the heart of God is not a comfortable package holiday, with a tour guide and every luxury laid on, but a 'road which passes through storms and desert wastes; through fire and flood; a road traversed by monsters and demons; a road fraught with danger'.[6] Tozer was certainly right when he wrote, 'The rare soul who presses on into the unusual experience reaches there after midnight.'[7] To enjoy God requires patience, submission, sacrifice and discipline. A 'quick-fit' spirituality will lead inevitably to disillusionment and self-deception.

Escapism

In spite of popular misconceptions, true devotion to God is never an escape from the rigours and pressures of modern living. The contemplative is often described as a desert dweller—as if he were some sort of 'deserter' from life! But in the desert of solitude, existence is stripped of all its trivialities and distractions; life is seen in its stark reality, exposed before the blistering light of God. True spirituality, therefore, is not the rejection of life, but its supreme affirmation; to meet God in solitude is to struggle with the evils that torment his world.

True spirituality is ultimately subversive. When we kneel to pray we begin a protest against the injustice of the world. To interpret the mission of the church in terms of a lifeboat rescuing people from a sinking ship can be misleading. God is not interested merely in rescuing the people, but in the salvage of the whole ship and its cargo. Bandit governments, oppressive laws, the pollution of the environment and the proliferation of nuclear weapons are issues close to God's heart.

Unfortunately, Satan always attempts to smear a style of Christianity that emphasises the importance of personal and corporate devotion, denigrating it as escapist, socially irrelevant, and self-obsessed. An historical example of Satan's intervention can be seen in the experience of the Pietists. Pietism was a spiritual movement that emerged a century after Luther. The Pietists reacted against the nominalism of the Lutheran Church, insisting on the importance of prayer, Bible study and personal piety. Their spirituality was not bogus but expressed itself in missionary endeavour and social action. Indeed, the Pietists placed such stress on good works that they were referred to derisively as 'Catholics'. H. Franke, for example, one of the leaders of the movement, established the world-famous Halle Foundation, an institution founded to promote charitable relief, social reform, education and evangelism. David Litz comments that this 'proved Pietism to be socially concerned, educationally innovative and global in vision'.[8] Ironically, the name 'pietist' has been prised out of context, and used as a synonym for subjective, world-renouncing spirituality. A movement that combined prayer with social action has been slandered, its name used derogatorily to describe a truly spiritual movement as a self-indulgent spirituality.

No tension should exist between the private life of prayer and public service. A study of the heroes of the Bible and church history reveals an undeniable relationship between deep personal piety and public achievement. Wilberforce, the social reformer and philanthropist, was a man of prayer. His antagonism towards slavery and his involvement with the abolition movement were a direct result of his commitment to Christ. Prayer and the study of the Bible were integral to his social vision. Whenever possible, Wilberforce retired to bed at 11 pm and rose at 6 am for prayer and meditation. Although by temperament impetuous and activistic, Wilberforce recognised the importance of self-examination. Pollock, a recent biographer, comments that 'with paper in front of him he would examine his motives, conduct and words. He had kept a brief daily journal; now he would often insert spiritual comments or confession, agonising over his sins.'[9] Regular confession and the scrutiny of his motives resulted in an almost exemplary public life. His politics were not the party politics of expediency and broken promises, but reflected his love for God and obedience to his word. 'A man who acts from the principles I profess,' he told a constituent, 'reflects that he is to give an account of his political conduct at the judgement seat of Christ.'[10]

It is evident that the piety of Wilberforce was not escapist. His private life with God found useful expression in the politics of his time. In 1833, the year of his death, the campaign of a lifetime was crowned with success: slavery was abolished in the British Empire. One of the most terrible injustices in history had been ended by a praying Christian.

Few of us have the ability and vocation of a Wilberforce, but a robust biblical spirituality will dramatically change our outlook and behaviour. It will affect our marriages, our relationships, our careers, our politics and our attitude and use of money. If this is not the case, our spirituality may be counterfeit.

Idolatry in disguise

At the heart of Christian experience is a paradox, for God is both known and unknown, revealed and mysterious. Our experience of God is rather like that of a partially sighted woman in a garden. Unable to focus properly on the delicate beauty of the flowers and shrubs, she sees the garden as if through a frosted glass window. The colours blend into each other, and the unique symmetry of each plant is lost in a myopic blur. By clumsily fitting these fragments of vision together, the woman may perhaps gain some idea of the loveliness of the garden. Similarly, our vision of God is imperfect, like a poor reflection in a mirror (1 Cor 13:12).

Inadequate vision can be further distorted by a theology of preference. Young children are noticeably faddy about food. Meals are often punctuated by such expressions as 'I hate cabbage. Take it away!' as the child throws it from the plate. After the child has been punished, he is lectured on the benefits of eating all his dinner. 'Cabbage is good for you,' remonstrates the parent. 'If you eat it all up, you'll be strong and clever.' Our attitude to God can be reminiscent of the behaviour of this child. We select those attributes of God's character that we find appealing, and reject those we find less attractive. Even the kind of spirituality that we prefer can be the result of unconscious preference. A complex, tortured type of person is more likely to gravitate towards the intense 'dark night' experience of John of the Cross or the existential theology of Søren Kierkegaard, while an extrovert may prefer the simple joy and delight of a Brother Lawrence or George Muller. Our choice of church, our family background and the general ethos and philosophy of our culture can also determine our view of God.

Unfortunately, there is no quick-fit solution to this problem. All of us carry extra emotional and cultural baggage that impedes our journey with God. The reshaping he undertakes in us is referred to as 'the renewing of the mind' (Rom 12:2; Eph 4:23). To enable this transformation, we must determine to submit to the authority of Scripture and allow it to impart a true portrait of God. Wrong images of God must be discarded, to be replaced by a more positive and scriptural view of the Creator.

If you are in doubt about my analysis, may I suggest a simple test. Write on a piece of paper everything you know about God. Adopt a shorthand approach. If, for example, you want to express the idea that God is love, don't write an essay on the subject, but merely put it down as a heading on the paper. When you have completed the exercise, consult with your spiritual director or a mature Christian and ask yourself the following questions:

1 Does my view of God equate with Scripture?
2 Are there emotional problems in my life that inhibit my relationship with God?
3 Has my church and/or theological training affected my view of God?
4 Is my view of God a reflection of my cultural preferences?
5 Am I temperamentally predisposed to prefer certain attributes of God to others?

I suspect that the response to these questions will be very interesting. The exercise may have exposed a subtle drift towards idolatry. A god of our own invention is far more accommodating than the dangerous and unpredictable God of the Bible. As we have seen, all of us have the propensity to dress God up in clothes that make him acceptable; take him to the cosmetic surgeon so his face fits our crowd, or send him to finishing school so he isn't a public embarrassment. The truth of revelation, however, prohibits such manipulation. God has not left us in perpetual night. He has revealed himself to us in the Scriptures. Surrender to God involves not only the acceptance of those attributes we find appealing, but of those attributes that are less palatable.

God is perfect in himself, whatever our personal preferences. To reflect on those attributes of his Being we find less attractive can enrich our lives enormously. The enjoyment of God is not something we control, like driving a fast car, but something that controls us. To throw wide the door to God is to invite a hurricane to enter.

Father has no favourites

God has no favourites. The intimacy with God that I have described in this book is for everyone. God is as willing to reveal himself to the secretary, the milkman, the schoolteacher and the housewife as he is to the religious 'professional'. Enjoyment of God is the legacy of all his people. If there is any élitism in the Bible, it is not based on the pretensions of a superior spiritual experience, but an inverted 'élitism' based on humble servanthood. Undoubtedly some within the church have greater maturity and live more closely to God, but this does not imply superiority. Many of the most godly people in the church are unknown. Furthermore, they are often as unconscious of their spirituality as Moses was of the glory that shone from his face (Ex 34:29). To suggest to them that they are in some way superior to the ordinary Christian would provoke either laughter or a firm rebuttal.

God desires the love and fellowship of each of his children. He is merely waiting for us to open our hearts to him and call out in longing. The enjoyment of God is for all of us.

The writing of this book has not been easy. As I sit here and reflect on my experience of God, I feel very much like a scuba diver exploring a coral reef. Tropical fish, as ethereal as dreams, hover over gardens of sea anemone, or soar above endless fantasies of coral. I am awed by the beauty of this submarine kingdom. The ocean stretches out before me in every direction: vast distances, unfathomable depths, hiding continents, deserts, mountain ranges, and jungles of dancing kelp—all waiting to be explored. The coral reef is only one of the many mysteries of the sea. My knowledge and experience are limited but I am driven on by the longing to know more. Thus I hope the lessons shared in this book have been helpful to you. God is worthy of our best. He calls us to live for him, to obey him, to explore him and enjoy him for ever.

God is the treasure of his people.

Notes

1 Johann Arndt, *True Christianity* (1720 edition), p 34.
2 Thomas Watson, *The Lord's Prayer* (Banner of Truth: London, 1972), p 275.
3 John Stott, *The Cross of Christ* (IVP: Leicester, 1986), p 187.
4 Dietrich Bonhoeffer, *The Cost of Discipleship* (SCM Press: London, 1959), p 35.
5 Cheslyn Jones, Geoffrey Wainwright, Edward Yarnold (eds), *The Study of Spirituality* (SPCK: London, 1986), p 42.
6 Kenneth Leech, *Spiritual and Pastoral Care* (Sheldon Press: London, 1986), p 6.
7 A.W. Tozer, *Born After Midnight* (Christian Publications: Harrisburg, Pennsylvania, 1959), p 10.
8 See 'Continental Pietism' in *The Study of Spirituality*, *op cit*, p 451.
9 John Pollock, *Wilberforce* (Lion: Tring, 1977), p 44–45.
10 *Ibid*, p 46.

Appendix: Questionnaire on the Devotional Life

1   How long do you spend with God each day?
2   What aids do you use in your time with God? (Bible notes etc.)
3   How do you manage your time to give quality time to God each day?
4   What methods do you adopt in Bible study, meditation and Bible reading? What benefits do you derive from these?
5   How do you organise your prayer time? (Please mention encouragements and difficulties that you encounter in prayer.)
6   Is silence before God an important part of your time with God? (Mention problems and benefits associated with silence.)
7   Do you have a family devotional time? If so, how do you convey to your children the enjoyment of knowing God?
8   In what ways does God speak to you? (Please give some practical illustrations.)
9   How do you maintain a close relationship with God throughout the day?
10 Does worship constitute an important part of your time with God? If so, how do you worship? (Singing, dancing, silent adoration, laughter etc.)
11 How many times a year, if any, would you go on a

spiritual retreat? (Please mention the benefits and problems associated with retreats.)

12 How does a satisfying and consistent devotional life affect your attitude to others, the church, evangelism and social involvement?

13 How regularly do you fast and what benefits do you derive from it?

14 Do you have mentor/mentors who counsel you on your devotional life? If the answer to the question is in the affirmative, what positive benefits do you derive from this guidance? If there are dangers, please mention these.

15 What books have helped you in your devotional life?

16 Is confession of sin a regular part of your Christian experience? Are there times when you engage in public confession? If so, what benefits do you derive from the public confession of sin?

17 What are the most common problems in your devotional life?

18 In a book on the devotional life, what topics do you think should be written about?

19 Please state your occupation.

To contact Andrew Brandon directly for speaking engagements or other purposes, write to:
Andrew Brandon
Christ for the World
PO Box 101, Stanmore, Middx HA7 1EW.

Loneliness

by Elisabeth Elliot

There is nothing unique about loneliness. We have all experienced it, overtaking us when we least expect it. Loneliness engulfs us whether we're married, not-yet-married, or used-to-be-married. It comes in all stages of our lives, and we suffer in it.

Loneliness (not solitude) is nevertheless a gift. Through its wilderness God blazes a pathway to holiness—even joy. In it we realise fully the glorious meaning of the Cross of Christ. By it God can transform our wilderness into a watered garden.

Twice widowed, three times married, and having worked as a missionary in the rain forests of Ecuador, Elisabeth Elliot knows loneliness well. But in this lyrical and perceptive book she leads us beyond loneliness...to hope.

Also by Elisabeth Elliot in Kingsway paperback: *The Glad Surrender*.

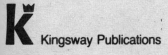

Kingsway Publications

Kingsway Publications

Kingsway Publications publishes books to encourage spiritual values in the home, church and society. The list includes Bibles, popular paperbacks, more specialist volumes, booklets, and a range of children's fiction.

Kingsway Publications is owned by The Servant Trust, a Christian charity run by representatives of the evangelical church in Britain, committed to serving God in publishing and music.

For further information on the Trust, including details of how you may be able to support its work, please write to:

> The Secretary
> The Servant Trust
> 1 St Anne's Road
> Eastbourne
> East Sussex BN21 3UN
> England